TWAYNE'S WORLD AUTHORS SERIES

A Survey of the World's Literature

Sylvia E. Bowman, Indiana University

GENERAL EDITOR

AUSTRIA

Ulrich Weisstein, Indiana University

EDITOR

ADALBERT STIFTER

(TWAS 274)

Adalbert Stifter

By MARGARET GUMP

Moravian College

Twayne Publishers, Inc.　: :　New York

ISBN 0-8057-2864-3

MANUFACTURED IN THE UNITED STATES OF AMERICA

FOR MY FAMILY

Preface

Although virtually unknown in this country outside a small circle of historians of German literature, Adalbert Stifter scarcely needs justification for being included in a World Authors Series. A bibliography of over 6,200 items, including translations into seventeen foreign languages, is to a writer what a halo is to a saint. Hermann Hesse has called Stifter the last classic of German prose, and the complete list of highly appreciative fellow craftsmen is impressive. Among Stifter's admirers besides Hesse are such famous writers as Nietzsche, Rilke, Thomas Mann, Hofmannsthal, and W. H. Auden.

The story of Stifter's fame, still to be written in its entirety, shows the fickleness of the reading public and the harm that firmly entrenched clichés can do. During his lifetime, his fame quickly rose to dizzy heights and then gradually declined. At the time of his death in 1868, his reputation as a writer had faded, and literary histories of the 1880's and 1890's granted him scant space in contrast to some mediocre writers, since forgotten. At the turn of the century, there occurred a Stifter renaissance. Its landmarks were the scholarly edition of his works (Prague, 1901ff.), Alois Raimund Hein's extensive biography (1904), Hermann Bahr's pamphlet, *Adalbert Stifter: Eine Entdeckung* (1919), and a series of excellent new popular editions of his works. Since that time, many German and Austrian scholars have dedicated their lives almost exclusively to Stifter research. But in English, apart from dissertations and articles in learned journals, there exists only one full-length book, Eric A. Blackall's critical study (1948), which presupposes, however, a knowledge of German. Unfortunately, many of Stifter's best stories and his two great novels have not yet been translated into English. The present study, therefore, aims to introduce this important writer to a larger public, stressing the unity of his life and work in his deep concern with man and his fate, as well as his emphasis on that which is good and right, on reason and humaneness. Since not all of Stifter's works can be treated at length, greater attention will be paid to those of the highest artistic merit which, at the same time, reveal his humanism most clearly. His essays and letters, enlightening though they are, cannot be treated separately and are referred to only occasionally to elucidate certain points.

Many individuals and institutions have helped me in the preparation of this study. I am especially indebted to the Adalbert Stifter-Institut in Linz and its director, Dr. Alois Groszschopf, for their valuable aid. I am also grateful for the generosity of the Upper Austrian government, which invited me to participate in the International Stifter Symposium at Bad Hall in 1968, the hundredth anniversary of Stifter's death. The dialogue with many prominent Stifter scholars proved most fruitful. To the personnel of the Moravian College Library I am indebted for procuring many books through interlibrary loan. But most of all, I want to express my deep gratitude to Dr. Dorothy Tyler, chairman of the Foreign Language Department at Moravian College, who read the manuscript and made many valuable suggestions.

MARGARET GUMP

Bethlehem, Pennsylvania

Contents

Chronology

1805   October 23: Adalbert Stifter born in Oberplan in southern Bohemia.
1817   November 21: father dies in an accident.
1818   November: Stifter enters the Gymnasium at the Benedictine Abbey of Kremsmünster in Upper Austria.
1826   Enrolls as a student of law at the University of Vienna.
1828   Falls in love with Fanny Greipl in Friedberg.
1833   Fanny's parents forbid further correspondence between the two young people.
1835   Stifter becomes engaged to Amalia Mohaupt.
1836   Fanny Greipl marries.
1837   Stifter marries Amalia Mohaupt.
1839   Fanny dies in childbirth.
1840   Publication of *Der Condor* and *Das Haidedorf.*
1841   *Feldblumen.—Die Mappe meines Urgrossvaters I.*
1842   *Der Hochwald.—Die Mappe meines Urgrossvaters II.—Die Sonnenfinsternis am 8.Juli 1842.*
1843   *Abdias.—Die Narrenburg.—Wirkungen eines weissen Mantels* (later: *Bergmilch*).
1844   *Wien und die Wiener.—Brigitta.—Die drei Schmiede ihres Schicksals.—Das alte Siegel.—Studien, vols. I and II.*
1845   *Der Hagestolz.—Der Waldsteig.—Der heilige Abend* (later: *Bergkristall*).
1846   *Die Schwestern.—Der beschriebene Tännling.*
1847   *Der Waldgänger.—Studien, vols. III and IV.*
1848   May, goes to Linz. *Prokopus.—Der arme Wohltäter* (later: *Kalkstein*).
1849   Final move to Linz. Editor of the *Linzer Zeitung.* Until February 1850 editor of the *Wiener Bote.* Political and cultural-political essays. *Die Pechbrenner* (later:*Granit*).
1850   Appointed *Schulrat* (supervisor) of elementary schools for Upper Austria. *Grosse goldene Medaille für Kunst und Wissenschaft.* Co-editor of the *Zeitschrift für österreichische Gymnasien.*—Political essays.—*Studien, vols. V and VI.*
1851   Reports about the *oberösterreichische Kunstverein* (1851–67).
1852   *Der Pförtner im Herrenhause* (later: *Turmalin*).
1853   *Bunte Steine.*

1854 *Ritterkreuz des Franz-Joseph-Ordens.* Together with Johannes Aprent: *Lesebuch zur Förderung humaner Bildung in Realschulen und in anderen zu weiterer Bildung vorbereitenden Mittelschulen.* Nervous disturbances.

1855 Increased nervous disturbances. First vacation.

1857 Journey to Klagenfurt and Trieste. *Der Nachsommer.*

¹858 Stifter's mother dies.

1859 Suicide of foster daughter Juliana Mohaupt.

1863 Beginning of fatal illness.

1864 Revision of *Die Mappe meines Urgrossvaters.—Nachkommenschaften.*

1865 Stifter is pensioned and nominated *Hofrat. Witiko, vol. I.*

1866 *Witiko, vol. II.—Der Waldbrunnen.—Der Kuss von Sentze.—Winterbriefe aus Kirchschlag.*

1867 Order of the White Falcon, bestowed by the Grand Duke Carl Alexander of Sachsen-Weimar. Work on the last version of *Die Mappe meines Urgrossvaters.—Witiko, vol. III.*—Completion of *Aus dem bairischen Walde* (published 1868).

1868 January 28, Adalbert Stifter dies.

CHAPTER 1

Biography

T HE life of Adalbert Stifter is, in many ways, typical of the artist
who does not fit into ordinary patterns and whose difficulties
and blunders are intimately connected with his genius. His life, apart
from the childhood and school years, was not happy. Hofmannsthal,
referring to Stifter's letters, comments:

What a tormented life that was, what a hopeless struggle, with no way of
managing with his pitiful official's salary; the everlasting sacrifice of the pure,
blessed hours of the day to the insipid, the superfluous, the trivial; his
childless, joyless marriage; the cruelty of losing through death all the creatures to whom he became attached. And those years in Austria, the mockery
of 1848, the catastrophe of 1859, the dismal catastrophe of 1866....[1]

But how few great artists have had "happy" personal lives! Their
happiness and misery are centered in the ecstasies and agonies of
artistic creation. Deeply troubled in his late twenties, Stifter cried
out, "I must produce and I shall" (*Br I,* 32).[2] And on December
22, 1860, after having produced the major part of his work, he said,
"I must write, or I shall die." A few years later, when he was already
a very sick man, his shattered nerves found bliss in revising his favorite work, *Die Mappe meines Urgrossvaters.*[3] Yet he knew, better
than any other writer except, perhaps, Flaubert, that writing is a
"hellish trade" because of the discrepancy between conception and
execution. He revised constantly and taxed to the utmost the patience
of publisher and printer alike. On June 8, 1861, he wrote to Gustav
Heckenast, his chief publisher and friend, "That is the tragedy of not
being able to achieve what one would like to. Yet this hellish trade
is sweeter and more alluring than office drudgery and life's struggle.
Even God can't change me now" (*Br III,* 284–85).

Stifter's external life was rather uneventful—"simple as a blade
of grass growing," as he says himself.[4] He was born in 1805, in
Oberplan, a village in southern Bohemia, now in Czechoslovakia,
but at that time part of the Austrian Empire. Stifter describes the
surrounding country as a landscape, "not charming, but quiet, silent
and almost epic" (*Br I,* 185). This landscape was an *Urerlebnis*

(elemental experience)[5] for him and forms the scenic background of much of his writing: misty blue mountains, reminiscent of those he could see from his father's house, appear at the horizon even in some stories whose setting is far from the Bohemian woods. Stifter's origins were humble. His father, trained as a linen weaver like his ancestors, changed to flax trading, combining it with small-scale farming. His mother was a butcher's daughter. In his works and letters, he speaks of both parents with filial piety. But since his father died when Stifter was very young, we know little of him except that he seems to have been a kind, quiet man who was fond of reading. Stifter always remained deeply attached to his mother. He called her "a woman with simple but deep and usually poetic feelings," "a rare human being." He believed that he inherited his basic disposition from her and that she, a woman without much formal education, was able to understand his works perfectly and effortlessly, whereas so many cleverer people sought the clues to them in vain.[6]

An exceptional village teacher, Jenne, discovered the boy's unusual intellectual gifts. Through him, Stifter learned to love great music, though music never played the same role as the visual arts in his life and work. To prepare the boy for further schooling, Jenne suggested Latin lessons with the local priest. But the priest considered him a completely inept pupil. Then, in 1817, the father was crushed to death by his overturned flax wagon, and the boy had to help his paternal grandfather with the farm work. There, in his own words, he began to feel "an infinite love for nature and solitude" (*Br I,* 185). That Stifter's schooling did not end with his father's death he owed to his maternal grandfather, who, in the summer of 1818, took him to the Benedictine abbey of Kremsmünster. Because of his deficiency in Latin, he might not have been admitted, but his examiner, Father Placidus Hall, later his teacher and benefactor, was impressed by the boy's amazingly exact knowledge of his home surroundings. He was accepted, entered in the fall, and stayed until 1826. He received excellent grades throughout and also many prizes. Very soon, he was able to earn money tutoring younger pupils. All his life he felt deep gratitude for Kremsmünster and called the years there "unquestionably the most beautiful of his life because they were the purest," an adjective which, for Stifter, always conveyed the highest praise (*Br VI,* 187).

Stifter's innate love of beauty must have found immense satisfaction in the splendid baroque buildings, art collections, and lovely surroundings, with the view of the Alps to the south and his native woods to the north. Extensive scientific collections, the observatory, and an outstanding science teacher helped him to develop his interests in this field. He had excellent teachers in all subjects and received good training in the classics, especially in Latin. He was also introduced to some of the great works of German literature. In the upper classes the students were asked to compose poetry. Stifter excelled there too, though without much originality either in the class exercises or in the verse he wrote on his own. He received good instruction in drawing and painting from Georg Riezlmayr, who first discovered the talent which Stifter cultivated the rest of his life. But most important in the Kremsmünster education was the general spirit prevailing there. It has been rightly called a blend of Enlightenment (of the period of the Emperor Joseph II), Catholicism, and humanism. There, according to Stifter's own testimony, his Weltanschauung and esthetic credo developed. As late as 1866, summarizing the influence of Kremsmünster, he wrote:

There . . . I first heard the statement that beauty is nothing but the divine presented in a beautiful form; that the divine is infinite in God but finite in man; that it is, however, the essence of his nature, striving everywhere for absolute revelation as the good, the true and the beautiful in religion, science, art, and human conduct—a revelation, which is the true source of man's happiness. This statement . . . struck forcibly the very core of my being, and all that followed in my life . . . led me to the same conclusion.[7]

The formative years in Kremsmünster left many traces in Stifter's work. Not by chance is the *Rosenhaus,* the center of his great novel, *Der Nachsommer,* placed in the countryside around Kremsmünster.

In 1826, Stifter went to Vienna to study law. Those interested in knowing how poor students lived at that time might read his humorous essay, "Leben und Haushalt dreier Wiener Studenten," in *Wien und die Wiener.* The university did not have the same impact on his mind as Kremsmünster; none of the professors there is mentioned by name in his later autobiographical sketches. Stifter passed all examinations but one; since he refused to take a reexamination, there was no formal conclusion to his studies and no academic degree. During his years at the university he realized that he was not meant to become a state official and that his chief interest lay in mathematics and science, which he studied on the side. It was impossible, however, to obtain a professorship in these fields, partly because his wide interests left no time to acquire the very specialized knowledge required for success in the competitive examinations leading to such a position.[8] But his broad learning made him a highly esteemed tutor in the cultured aristocratic and upper-middle-class circles of Vienna. He had a natural gift for teaching and tried to educate his pupils while teaching them. Here, as in his writings, his strong ethical and didactic bent found expression. He was well liked by his pupils and their parents, and many homes were opened to him. Considering his excellent rapport with so many pupils and parents and the fact that his activity as a tutor was the gateway to the best Viennese society, it is rather astonishing to find in Stifter's writing a bitter remark on the humiliating status of a tutor: he is really not better thought of than a juggler, scorned for having to sell his skills.[9] Certainly Stifter made many friends during those early years in Vienna, and many of his most intimate friends belonged to the nobility. It is interesting to note that they were considerably younger than he. Later, in 1842 and 1843, when he was already known as a writer, he was employed as reader to Princess Maria Anna von Schwarzenberg, an unusually intelligent and liberal-minded woman, and was frequently invited to visit her after his employment had ended. And from 1843 to 1846, he instructed Metternich's son, Richard, in physics and mathematics. Stifter thus gained a firsthand knowledge of aristocratic manners which was helpful to him in writing *Der Nachsommer*.

While Stifter was a student, he always spent his summer vacations at home in Oberplan. A good part of the time, however, was spent in the nearby town of Friedberg, where he had friends. There he fell in love with Fanny Greipl, the gentle, attractive daughter of a well-to-do merchant. His letters give us a fairly clear picture of his conduct during their relationship. There is a curious, almost neurotic vacillation between his desire and determination to win her as his wife, in spite of his uncertain financial status, and resignation to her being beyond his reach. His application for a professorship in physics at the University of Prague, his taking the written examination but failing to appear at the oral one, seem symptomatic. In response, Fanny's parents, never much in favor of this "unsuitable" suitor, let him know through her brother that they wished no further correspondence. Meanwhile, in the winter of 1832–33, or perhaps earlier, Stifter had made the acquaintance of a young milliner, Amalia Mohaupt, who was poor but exceptionally beautiful. That he, now a man of twenty-seven and so much in love with Fanny, could not resist this sensuous infatuation gave him a permanent feeling of guilt and explains much of his later condemnation of passion and the almost complete absence of any sensuousness in his love scenes. In a letter to a young friend, he juxtaposes his two loves: "If the one girl inflames, enraptures and damns, there lies in the eye of the other a charm which absolves, calms the storms. . . . On my prostituted lips, her gentle, innocent, warm kiss burns like purgatory." He speaks of himself as a rascal who should be whipped with 93 sleigh whips. Two years later there followed a letter of confession in which he tried to win Fanny back. He speaks of her "innocent chaste heart on which he would like to unburden himself in bitter tears." She always was for him "the bride of his soul," "the saint to whom his better self prayed." He tells her that he broke with Amalia because "I did not love her and in order to enjoy her kiss, I had to think of *your* lips."[10] This is painful to read and must have hurt Fanny to the quick. She did not answer, and in 1837 Stifter married Amalia.

Much has been written about her and their marriage. She was neither the monster which some of his biographers make of her, nor the wonderful, almost saintly person into which Stifter transfigured her in his late letters. Most people who knew her describe her as rather cold, buttoned-up, hard to get along with, miserly, and obsessed with cleanliness and orderliness. If some of these testimonies are perhaps biased, there are still the photographs, which confirm the impression of a rather unfriendly, not very lovable person. She has been compared to Goethe's Christiane, with whom she shared physical beauty, humble social background, and the inability to take any real interest in her husband's work. Unfortunately for Stifter, she lacked Christiane's vitality and cheerfulness. She seems to have been nervous and irritable. Nevertheless, Stifter's late letters are sincere in spite of their strangely exaggerated and constant affirmation of his love for her and her good qualities. Some of this was undoubtedly caused by a feeling of guilt that he had made her suffer so much through his illness and reads like a promissory note to be honored in the future when they would live together in harmony, undisturbed by their respective shortcomings. They had no children, and Stifter, in his growing loneliness, needed somebody he could love, idolize, worry about, write to, someone who cared for him—in the double meaning of the word. And that Amalia did. She gave him a comfortable, well-kept home, nursed him in his illness (not an easy task),[11] and, if she could not share his intellectual life, they could share their love of dogs, paintings, and antiques. Gustav Wilhelm is probably right in stating that, at least for the last years of Stifter's life, one can speak neither of tragedy nor of halcyon happiness in their marriage (*Br V,* XVII).

The couple began their married life in Vienna very modestly, for Stifter was often in financial straits. His income was based solely on private tutoring and the occasional sale of a painting. Then, in 1840, his first story, *Der Condor,* was published and was an immediate success. A period of great literary productivity followed. Strangely enough, at this time Stifter thought of himself chiefly as a painter, even after the breakthrough of *Abdias* in 1843 and the publication of the first two volumes of the *Studien* in 1844.[12] His rank as a painter is indeed far above that of a "Sunday painter"—he has some excellent paintings to his credit.[13] But there is no doubt that he was greater as a writer. It is also a fact that his gift as a painter influenced his writings more than has been true of other men with double talents: Goethe or Gottfried Keller, for example. On the other hand, Stifter's double gift has led to an almost ineradicable misinterpretation of his writings. It was so easy to label him, once and for all, "a painter with the pen," capable of describing beautiful landscapes, but not of creating interesting human characters, not to mention interesting plots.[14]

The most important event during Stifter's stay in Vienna was the Revolution of 1848. He himself considered it a dividing line in his life, saying that he had been "serene like the people of classical antiquity (at least until 1848)" (*Br II,* 94). We know that, at first, he greatly rejoiced in the newly won freedom, although not without misgivings for the future (*Br VII,* 57–58, 301). He was a delegate from his district to the preparatory meetings for the Frankfurt parliament. But he was soon deeply shocked at the turn which the revolution took in the violent uprisings of May and October. In the new radicalism he saw forces at work which seemed to destroy everything he believed in: morals, art, the sacred, the divine. His idea of freedom, the concurrence of moral and political freedom, had not been realized. Moral freedom meant for Stifter the supremacy of reason, complete self-control, freedom from personal passions and desires, from lust of power. In an often-quoted letter to Hecke-nast (May 25, 1848), he calls himself a man of moderation and freedom and, shifting the emphasis from the political to the ethical sphere, regrets the liberation of passions. He believed in the power of the "controlled, noble, quiet word, which, however, sheds light on all sides," "the gentle olive branch." All this shows that he had no understanding of the revolutionary process, of the fact that pressures long endured will produce volcanic eruptions and that the pendulum inevitably swings far to the other side. What he had really wished for was evolution, not revolution.[15] He viewed everything from the lofty peak of the classical eighteenth-century *Humanitäts-ideal,* without looking closely at existing political, and especially social, conditions. He was not alone in this; many writers, Grill-parzer among them, and the liberal *Bürgertum* as a whole, reacted very similarly. That in 1848 the German *Humanitätsideal* failed in the actual sphere of politics was a tragedy for Austria and Germany. In his deep disappointment, Stifter saw the only salvation in education *(Bildung),* equating moral with political freedom. On March 6, 1849, he wrote:

The ideal of freedom has been destroyed for a long while to come. He who is morally free, can be politically free; actually he always is. No power on earth can make a man free otherwise. There is only one force which can effect that: *education (Bildung).* Therefore I began to feel a desperate longing: "Let the little ones come unto me"; for only through them, if the state takes their education and humanization (*Menschwerdung*) into its enlightened hands, can reason, that is, freedom, be established; otherwise never.[16]

Reasoning that the people had to be educated to a higher moral and intellectual level *(Vernunftentwicklung)* before one could grant them full political freedom, Stifter, in a series of newspaper articles, sided with the government, a position for which he has been taken to task in our time.[17] Many of his articles were exclusively con-cerned with educational reforms and the moral improvement of the people. It was, therefore, appropriate that eventually, in June 1850, he was appointed *Schulrat,* that is, supervisor of the *Volksschulen* (elementary schools) for Upper Austria. Linz, its capital, had been his permanent residence since the spring of 1848, and he had already served in an advisory capacity to the governor of Upper Austria.

In reading about Stifter's years in Linz after his appointment as *Schulrat,* one is immediately struck by the scope and variety of his work. After grueling days of school examinations, he spent hours on his writing, or he got up at four in the morning to write before the official day began. He had no vacation during the first five years. While on school inspection trips, he became interested in the preservation of old churches and altars, and in December 1853, he was appointed curator of art and historical monuments for Upper Austria. His best-known achievement in this capacity (actually started before 1853) is the restoration of the Gothic altar in Kefermarkt (Kerberg altar in *Der Nachsommer*). He was a member and then vice-president of the *Linzer Kunstverein,* for which he wrote the exposition reviews; he was also a member of the executive committee and special consultant of the State Museum of Upper Austria. His hobbies were time-consuming: painting, to which he always returned after long intervals; restoring pictures and antique furniture; and raising cacti.[18]

Stifter began his work as *Schulrat* with enthusiam and enjoyed it very much at first. Critics who reproach him for lack of social concern are ignorant of the details of this part of his life. His reports show that he was painfully aware of the abject poverty of the teachers and their humiliatingly low social status. He was also concerned about their insufficient preparation, which he tried in vain to change thoroughly. He was, however, very successful in obtaining better school buildings. In January 1854, there were in Upper Austria 133 school buildings either new, remodeled, or in the building or planning stage.[19] But fairly soon Stifter began to feel that his writing suffered because of his duties as *Schulrat.* (He mentions this fact at the end of 1851.) At the outset, it was not so much that he begrudged the time, as that the trivia of his profession crowded out his poetic visions. He spoke with envy of Goethe, who found in his prince an understanding patron, whom he repaid with immortal works. He overlooked the fact that Goethe, too, suffered deeply at times under the burdens imposed upon a state minister.[20] As the years passed, Stifter's strength diminished, and he suffered great disappointments and slights.[21] His laments became more frequent, anguished, and bitter. He was less and less satisfied with what he could accomplish for the benefit of mankind as an official compared with what he could do as a poet, and he felt that he had betrayed his muse. He called his work "unfruitful" (1855), "repugnant" (1857), "tormenting slave labor" (1859). He ardently longed to be freed from it, constantly mentioned his plans for his deliverance. But he could not relinquish his post; he desperately needed his pitiful salary.

During all his years in Linz, Stifter was in a difficult financial position; he had to sell the copyright to *Studien* and *Bunte Steine*, thus depriving himself of any income from later editions. He constantly had to ask Heckenast for advances on the agreed monthly rates and had to borrow money from other people besides. His official position forced him to keep up appearances and to give more to charity than his income warranted. (His heart also drove him to that.) He loved good food and wines and, above all, beautiful things. He bought good paintings and exquisite antique furniture, "fit for an emperor's room,"²² all of which he could ill afford. Like Balzac, he had no luck with his efforts to escape from financial straits: he lost on stocks he had Heckenast buy for him; he never won in the State Lottery; and the anthology *(Lesebuch zur Förderung humaner Bildung)*, which he published together with his friend Aprent, was turned down by the Ministry of Education. For lack of money he could not travel very far. In 1857, he managed to get to Trieste, not without going into debt, however. The ocean, which he had never seen before, the Italian landscape, the people, the beauty of it all, transported him. "With this little foretaste," he writes back in Linz, "I often felt as if I should weep bitterly that I have become so old and had not seen that." He knew for certain that, another time, he would stay longer in Italy, live perhaps for years in Rome. Again he mentioned Goethe who, he said, had become a great poet only through Italy *(Br III,* 36–40). How little he knew what lay ahead! With his fame declining, his illness and the great expenses it brought, his financial situation worsened. The last letter he wrote (six days before his death) is an anguished outcry for help, directed to his old friend Heckenast:

I implore you in the name of everything sacred in our friendship, which has always been so close, not to forsake me in the present misery of my family. Everything will come out right again. You will set up a monument for yourself and for me, and your son, I am sure, will reap the profits. *(Br VI,* 182)

There were other misfortunes that affected him more deeply than his chronic financial difficulties. In 1846, Gustav Scheibert, a young friend whom he considered almost a son, died after a brief illness. In 1847, the Stifters adopted Amalia's six-year-old niece Juliana. The child proved difficult—whether Amalia treated her properly has been questioned—and ran away when she was not quite eleven years old. In 1859, she committed suicide by drowning herself in the Danube. A distant relative, Josefine Stifter, a very lovable girl whom he had also taken into his home, had to be sent away in 1858 because of tuberculosis, and she died in 1859. After Juliana's and Josefine's death, Stifter wrote: "Thus we are alone again, two lonely, aging people." The loss of his brother's two small children in 1857 and 1862 also grieved him deeply. Finally the death of his dog (in 1862), his beloved companion for nine years, brings out the poignancy of Hofmannsthal's comment on Stifter's loss of every creature to whom he became attached.

At the end of 1863, Stifter himself became very ill. There had been forewarnings, which he had ignored. His illness has been diagnosed as cancer or cirrhosis of the liver, and recently also as tuberculosis. Suffice it to say that he suffered a great deal, especially mentally, from restlessness, irritability, depression, anxiety, and various phobias. A photograph taken in the last years of his life shows a once portly man now wasted away. Some biographers deny that these mental symptoms had anything to do with his physical ailment, a view which seems to me highly debatable. Although there were longer or shorter respites from illness, Stifter never completely recovered. After a long leave of absence, he was finally pensioned in November 1865. The pension came too late to let him fully enjoy the long-hoped-for leisure, but he could at least finish his last great novel, *Witiko*. In December 1867, he fell seriously ill once more, and in the night of January 25–26, he inflicted a wound on his throat with a razor blade. The doctor was able to sew the wound together, and Stifter lived on for more than fifty hours. The wound probably accelerated, but was not the real cause of, his death. Unless new documents turn up, it may never be known how lucid Stifter was when he wounded himself and whether or not one can actually speak of suicide, which Stifter considered a "moral crime." But it seems futile and relatively unimportant to speculate further on the question.[23] Whatever the answer, we should not interpret his life and work retroactively from his death as nothing but a bright superstructure above a dark abyss. We must understand him from what he had to say in his works and letters and shall find that he was neither the serene man of childlike faith that the early critics saw in him nor the wholly pathological figure depicted by some of the more recent ones.

CHAPTER 2

Studien: *Volumes I to III*

THE *Studien* are the first collection of Stifter's *Novellen*, published in six volumes between 1844 and 1850: Volumes I and II in 1844, Volumes III and IV in 1847, Volumes V and VI in 1850. All of them had previously appeared in various publications.[1] The title is misleading: with the exception of the first two stories, one could not possibly call them studies or sketches. Even for the first two pieces the title is not really appropriate. The Preface, justifying the title, is a choice example of Stifter's self-disparagement, which so strangely alternates with a belief in his high rank as a writer. But whatever his self-evaluation, here as elsewhere, he stresses the ethical purpose of his writing.[2] Stifter carefully reworked the stories for the *Studien*. It is these versions, familiar to the general reader, which will be used in this discussion, with reference to the first versions whenever necessary.[3]

The first of the *Studien, Der Condor,* is the story of a young painter, Gustav R., and his pupil Cornelia, a proud young woman of the upper class. In order to prove that women are equal to men, she takes part in the flight of a balloon named Condor.[4] She fails in her attempt, because she becomes ill, and the balloon has to descend prematurely, to the great disappointment of the two scientists who originated the flight. This experience changes Cornelia: she becomes more humble and feminine, *"gut und sanft"* (good and gentle), in Stifter's favorite words. The two young people then find each other in a love scene which also constitutes their farewell. Gustav's sudden decision to set out, next day, on a previously planned journey is rather awkward and unconvincing. The last chapter of the story recounts Cornelia's visit to an exhibition in Paris, where two of Gustav's pictures are shown. She cannot tear herself away from them. She has lost Gustav through her own fault, probably by not being able to resist the allurement of being the center of society's admiration. The fact that we do not learn what has happened between the two lovers shows the uncertain hand of the novice writer. It is characteristic of Stifter's conception of the artist that no blame for their separation is put on Gustav. He has sublimated his sorrow in his work: the softly shimmering light on his *innocent, chaste* pictures affects Cornelia like a mute but permanent reproach.[5] Gustav *is* the artist Stifter would have liked to be.

In spite of its beauty, the story seems dated. This is ironical, for it is the only one in which Stifter, so often reproached for avoiding contemporary problems, actually deals with one, namely the emancipation of women. In our era of female astronauts, we cannot help smiling when we read a sentence like "Women cannot endure the heavens" (I, 23 and 29).[6] Stifter, who in later years spoke sharply against any *littérature engagée,* may already have felt the danger of becoming outmoded. In the *Studien* version, he wisely omits Gustav's parting words: *"Cornelia, werde ein Weib!"* (Cornelia, be a woman!) To the modern reader, this sounds downright comical.

The merit of the story lies undoubtedly in Stifter's unique gift for evoking visual images: Vienna in the moonlight, the changing colors of space (foreshadowing the later, famous description in "Die Sonnenfinsternis am 8. Juli 1842"), the cords of the balloon contrasting in the flaming morning sun with the indigo blue of the sky, Cornelia's white satin gown set off against the dark green leaves of the camelia plant. It cannot be denied that in *Der Condor* Stifter has not freed himself from Romantic influences, especially those of Jean Paul and E.T.A. Hoffmann: the excessive use of moonlight, exalted feelings, the subjective diary form of the first chapter, the dialogue with the tomcat Hinze, the notes, and the sometimes bizarre metaphors. But for the attentive reader, many passages are already unmistakably Stifterian.

The next story in the *Studien, Feldblumen,* shows the influence of Jean Paul even more strongly, especially in the first version. In addition to some of the characteristics mentioned above, there is the device of symbolic chapter headings, undoubtedly taken from Jean Paul's *Flegeljahre.*[7] *Feldblumen* consists of eighteen letters in diary form which the painter Albrecht sends to his friend Titus in the Pyrenees. (The nineteenth chapter is written by the narrator of the story.) One is reminded of Goethe's *Leiden des jungen Werthers* when Albrecht indulges his feelings, bares his heart to his faraway friend, spends his day at a favorite spot in the open, and befriends simple people and children. The eighteenth-century Werther, in Rousseauistic fashion, it is true, picks his peas

himself and cooks them on the kitchen stove of the inn, whereas
Stifter's more bourgeois nineteenth-century hero has his meal served
to him. Another even more important difference is that in Goethe's
Werther we learn more about the recipient of the letters, whose
sharply contrasting character brings Werther into stronger relief.

As in *Werther,* and probably in most stories written in letter
form, there is relatively little action in *Feldblumen.* Albrecht falls
in love with Angela, a young woman of unconventional upbringing.
He becomes engaged to her, but on the following day, he takes
an early morning walk in the park of Schönbrunn, where he finds
his beloved in tender conversation with a stranger. In a fit of blind
jealousy, he leaves for the Alps. The stranger, who really is Emil,
Angela's foster brother and former teacher, follows him there.
He too loves Angela, but renounces her selflessly when he learns
about Albrecht. Angela forgives Albrecht, and in the last chapter
she is his happy wife. Emil's sister, Natalie, has married Albrecht's
friend, Lothar. Stifter restrains himself from ending the story with
more than two couples, but there is a hint of a third one, and all's
well that ends well.

When Stifter later wrote *Der Hochwald,* he found fault with
the agitation and capriciousness of *Feldblumen.*[8] The story could,
therefore, be dismissed as unimportant for a discussion of Stifter's
work if it did not reflect so much of Stifter's life in the 1830's and
if some of his main themes were not treated here for the first time:
dreams of an ideal home and an ideal wife, and above all, the condemnation of passion as something intrinsically bad. Angela represents the ideal woman about whom Stifter wrote in such exalted
terms in letters to his friends but whom he had not found in real
life. She possesses a keen intellect, deep feeling, utmost purity, and
is, therefore, independent of social conventions. Her education,
partly modeled on that of Stifter's private pupils, includes the study
of French and English, Greek and Latin, mathematics, natural
sciences (with the exception of physiology, which she feared would
destroy her beautiful inner world!), psychology, natural law *(Natur-
recht),* philosophy, and history. But she is not a bluestocking; she
can even cook, and domestic and intellectual qualities blend in
her delightfully. Although in *Feldblumen,* in contrast to *Der Condor,*
Stifter advocates a partial emancipation of women, he does not rise
completely above the ideas of his time. It is true that he grants a

woman the right to exist for her own sake, but one could almost overlook this grand gesture because it is preceded by a short discourse on her preparation for being a good mother and is followed by a statement of the qualities needed to make her future husband happy. Angela is chaste, good, kind, gentle, and forgiving. She possesses classical beauty, like Natalie in *Der Nachsommer*. Her unusually big eyes, black as lava, are passionate, yet her glance is as chaste as a madonna's! It is Albrecht's unreasonable, and therefore in Stifter's eyes unforgivable, jealousy that jeopardizes for a moment the possession of such treasures as Angela and the idyllic retreat he wants to create by a lake for the two of them and some friends.

This ideal community, whose aim it is to establish the rule of reason on earth, would punish by exile any person succumbing to crude passion. What strikes the reader of *Feldblumen,* knowing Stifter's later work, is his early emphasis on the ethical, on the qualities of purity, kindness, gentleness, simplicity, and nobility of soul. Words such as *einfach, einfältig* (simple), *rein* (pure), *keusch* (chaste), *unschuldig* (innocent), *fromm* (good), *sanft* (gentle), *sittlich* (moral), and *edel* (noble) appear on almost every page. These words can be only approximately translated. There is overlapping in meaning; for instance, *fromm* means pious, innocent, good, and gentle; *rein* means both clean and pure. Cleanliness of appearance is for Stifter a symbol of purity of heart. White clothing, the whiteness and purity of linen are used symbolically throughout his work. The highest praise given to any person in *Feldblumen* is that he or she is innocent, good, gentle, and selfless. These qualities, always the basis for mutual love, make Stifter's heroes sometimes pale and bloodless. The *Studien* version of *Feldblumen* goes even further than the first one in not allowing any sensuousness or passion to show its ugly head. Thus, in the first version Albrecht and Angela kiss each other in the engagement scene, while in the *Studien* version he merely kisses her hand. In both versions, in the eleventh letter, a revealing distinction is made between love as sexual passion and the nobility of true love. Stifter's remorse for having given up a Fanny Greipl for an Amalia Mohaupt is all too apparent in *Feldblumen*. In his work, he wanted to ignore "human bondage."

With the third story of the first volume, *Das Haidedorf* (The Village on the Heath), Stifter has come into his own.[9] Although one short passage of *Feldblumen* conveys a nostalgic longing for the solemn Sunday morning of his childhood, *Das Haidedorf* is the first story which has its roots in Stifter's childhood and native landscape. In contrast to the *Stimmungsbilder* (impressionistic scenes) in *Feldblumen,* Stifter here for the first time re-creates a particular landscape, the so-called Heath near Oberplan, and the Rossberg, a small elevation in it. For the first time also he re-creates one of those unpretentious, rather bare landscapes to which he was so partial. In order to bring out the peculiar beauty of such a landscape, Stifter had to use an oxymoron: "a sadly charming little piece of soil" *(ein traurig liebliches Fleckchen Landes).* Here, for the first time, he pictures the work and joy of the peasant, the same throughout millennia, the life of each being a link in an unending chain, the chain a symbol of continuity, each link a symbol of the transitoriness of human existence. For the first time, he depicts the simple life of just, hard-working people, guided by the "gentle law," a life which, in the Preface to *Bunte Steine,* he was to call greater than that of heroes. Here, as in *Die Mappe, Brigitta, Zwei Schwestern,* and *Der Nachsommer,* people prosper through the example, help, and advice of an experienced and progressive neighbor. Here, for the first time, he presents an ideal family, whose members are united in deep love and mutual concern, although, in the manner of peasants, they are embarrassed and ashamed of showing their feelings. The little shepherd boy Felix is a slightly idealized version of the boy Stifter. From a letter to his brother Anton we know that he had his own father and mother in mind when he created the lovable figures of the parents (*Br I,* 129). But the most remarkable character is, without doubt, the grandmother, for whom Stifter's own grandmother, Ursula Kary, was the model. In the story, she is over a hundred years old, "living on eternally to an age beyond comprehension, like someone forgotten by death." Her lonely figure, sitting in the sun and communing with her dead, or kneeling and praying in the meadow behind the house, is one of the leitmotifs in the story. In her are mingled dotage and spiritual strength. Biblical figures are as near to her as the now dead companions of her long life. And it is she who first kindles the divine spark in the boy who listens to her stories, feeling them more than understanding them; it is she as well who first recognizes that he has become a poet during his long absence from home.

Felix's poetic mission brings him bliss and pain—the unspeakable bliss of creation and the loss of ordinary human happiness. The father of the woman he loves, although a friend of his, refuses to give him his daughter in marriage because of "the position he has chosen in the world"—as if the poet had a choice.[10] But Felix is resigned to his fate. While he waits for an answer to his request for the girl's hand, the villagers ardently wish for rain. He tells his father that their hope will be fulfilled (he has learned to interpret the signs of the sky), but not his own hope: "God's ways are always, always right even when he sends sorrow and renunciation." Felix's resignation to the will of God is paralleled by his father's confidence in God's wisdom. When the father had momentarily considered using the abundant juniper berries to feed the domestic animals, he worried about the birds and the deer. But then he thought that the Lord would suggest to them other sources of food. The father reflects Stifter's deliberately optimistic, unquestioning piety which refuses to see the cruel struggle for existence in nature.

The answer to Felix's fervent wish, and to that of the peasants, comes at almost the same time; his a negative one on the eve of Pentecost; theirs a positive one on Pentecost itself. A steady, gentle rain ends the drought, and the people, joyously walking through the rain, go to church to thank God. Felix is among them, thanking God too, and nobody knows what his gentle, quiet eyes conceal.

In *Das Haidedorf*, even more than in *Feldblumen*, there is emphasis on gentleness, kindness, goodness, to the exclusion of any utterance of loud and violent passion. There is also great, perhaps excessive, emphasis, on innocence and purity. The boy Felix is as innocent and pure as the flowers and little animals, his first companions and educators. In Stifter's opinion, the child, naturally good, will remain good if we do not interfere. This short passage about education (I, 177) reads like unadulterated Rousseau. It is interesting to note here that Stifter, in all his work, never pictures "naughty" children. During the journeys which take Felix far away from his Heath, he matures but remains good and chaste. His goodness and purity are apparent to his mother and father and the villagers. In the first version of the story, in characteristic fairy-tale fashion, Stifter has the king come to the village and honor Felix as a famous poet before the overawed family and the other village people. As an "honored and justified man" (*Urf. I,* 168), he stands before those who had looked upon him as a stranger with a mixture of curiosity and awe. He refuses to accept the jewels which the king offers him and asks only for help for the village people. It is not difficult to see that Stifter would have liked to come home to his village in such a triumph. In the *Studien* version, his artistic sense made him reduce this obvious vicarious recognition to a few hints. Here Felix has some influence with the authorities in the capital; he has rich friends there, and he himself could help if necessary. (In the later story, *Die Mappe,* the main protagonist, also a peasant's son, gains recognition as a skilled physician in his native woods.)

The style of *Das Haidedorf* is much more subdued than that of *Der Condor* and *Feldblumen.* There are fewer metaphors, fewer ejaculations and intrusions by the author. The sentences flow quietly and melodiously. It is as if the simplicity, stillness, and serenity of the Heath had communicated itself, not only to the persons, but to the language as well. A poetic luster shining throughout makes us accept this unshadowed purity to which we might otherwise object.

With *Der Hochwald* (The Primeval Forest), the first piece in the second volume of the *Studien* and one of his best-known stories, Stifter has come into full possession of his powers as a writer. He himself realized that he had made a great step forward since *Feldblumen,* and without being completely satisfied, began to know his own worth. For the first time he thinks of Goethe in comparison with himself, still placing himself far below Goethe, however.[11] He had originally planned to call this story *Der Wildschütz* (The Poacher) and had changed the title because here the forest is more than mere background for the story. It is, in a sense, one of the protagonists, and the chapters appropriately bear the names of *Waldburg, Waldwanderung, Waldhaus, Waldsee, Waldwiese, Waldfels, Waldruine.* Either the forest is in harmony with human feelings and events or its solitude, stillness, and peace contrast with the turbulent, destructive ways of man.

As in many of his stories, Stifter begins with a description of the setting: the Plöckenstein Lake, hidden in an almost inaccessible part of the Bohemian woods, a landscape of melancholy beauty, and the ruins of the castle Wittinghausen, which can be seen from the little town of Friedberg. There, as he tells us, he had dreamed the double dream of youth and first love, and we possess paintings and drawings of both scenes by his own hand.

Although the story takes place during the Thirty Years War, the emphasis is not on historical facts. Much later, when Stifter was working on his great historical novel *Witiko,* he deplored his fanciful treatment of history in *Der Hochwald.*[12] The Lord of Witinghausen, father of two motherless daughters, Clarissa and Johanna, has a house built at Plöckenstein Lake to protect them from the dangers of war. He takes them there, entrusting them to the custody of a friend of his youth, Gregor. Both men are old now, the one formed by a long life of knighthood, the other—"a brother of the rock"—by a long life with nature. It is Gregor, a simple farmer, who becomes the center of interest. He has spent most of his later life in the forest and is now one with it. It speaks to him; it feels and can be hurt like a human being. He will not allow live trees to be cut down to provide firewood; the house, built as a refuge in the hitherto untouched wilderness, has to be destroyed afterward and the place, its "heart," given back to the forest. He speaks out against an arrogant, anthropocentric conception of nature. Plants and animals are his brethren, as they are for Goethe's Faust.[13] For Gregor, the reverence for life, to use Albert Schweitzer's term, extends to all life, since all life comes from God. He will not accept as true the legends his grandmother has told him because, as he says, the forest does not effect "evil" miracles, but only "quiet and insignificant" ones, which in reality are much greater: those caused by the slow action of water, earth, air, and sunshine. But man cannot understand those miracles and substitutes his own coarser explanations. This anticipates Stifter's Preface to *Bunte Steine: "gross"* (great) and *"klein"* (small) are human terms, not immanent in the cosmic order. Another point about natural order is made by Gregor when he and the two sisters see a beautiful hawk circling slowly above the lake. Gregor defends the bird against the "people out there" who call it a "beast of prey." It is, he says, as innocent as the lamb which feeds on innocent herbs and flowers: "It must have been thus ordered in the world that one being lives at the expense of another," Gregor concludes, carefully avoiding mention of the anguish and suffering inherent in this "order" (I, 261 f.). There is, as we have already seen in *Das Haidedorf,* a blind spot in Stifter's view of nature, which is all the more significant since it did not spring from ignorance.[14]

Weeks go by and nothing disturbs the peace of the woods, as if

there were no war. From the top of the Plöckenstein mountain, with
the aid of a telescope, the sisters can see the tower of their castle,
a small neat blue square; and the news from home is good. Their
anxiety vanishes, and with the help of their mentor Gregor, the soul
and poetic voice of the forest, they begin to feel and love its unspeakable beauty. Nature reciprocates: she receives them as her own, as
if they were elves. However, this peace is rudely interrupted one
day while the girls, together with Gregor, sit lazily at the lake enjoying the warmth of Indian summer and admiring the beauty of
the hawk. A sudden shot brings the bird down. The noise is all the
more terrifying since it had been so uncannily quiet. It is the first
foreboding of what is to come. When Gregor takes the bullet from
the hawk's body, he knows the marksman. It is his young friend
Ronald who fired the shot so that Gregor would know of his presence. Ronald has loved Clarissa since her childhood, and to her he
makes himself known through an old song he used to sing when he
lived at her father's castle. Clarissa arranges a meeting with him,
to which Johanna and Gregor must accompany her. She had tried
to conquer her "sinful" passion for Ronald but is again completely
overwhelmed by his presence, just as when she was a child. Ronald
is a fairy-tale prince, blond, blue-eyed, extremely handsome, roman-
tically gentle and adventurous at the same time. He is an illegitimate
son of the Swedish King Gustavus Adolphus and wants to use his
influence with the Swedish army to save Wittinghausen and Clarissa's
father and young brother. He would like to linger a while, because
he too feels enchanted by the still air, the warm autumn sun, and
the peace of the woods. He feels as if he had changed, as if there
were no *"Draussen"* (outside world) with its war and destruction,
but only people who love each other and learn innocence from the
innocence of the forest. But after calling upon nature to witness the
sacred vows which he and Clarissa exchange, he tears himself away.
After his departure, everything appears to be the same, but "Clarissa
was no longer calm—Johanna no longer happy."

Late fall sets in, sad, yet indescribably beautiful. "And when the
girls sat silently, looking out into the woods, there was a soft rustling
beside them and one or two leaves of a wild cherry tree, red as blood,
fell at their feet. They sat there, watching the spectacle, autumnally
sad themselves" (I, 296). The inevitable happens. The change in the
woods prepares the reader for what is to come. The red and yellow

colors of the foliage form bloody stripes running through the dark
fir woods. Through the telescope, the girls and Gregor see a little
cloud instead of the familiar blue square of their tower. The next
day, they again climb the Plöckenstein and realize that frost has
wrought more havoc in the woods. Another look through the telescope shows the destruction of their home: the tower no longer has
a roof, and fire has left dark spots in the walls. The only thing which
has not changed is the serene, sparkling sky above, which makes
the destruction all the harder to accept.

In the last chapter, we meet Clarissa and Johanna in the ruins
of their castle. They learn from the knight Bruno, who loves Clarissa
with a steadfast but unrequited love, what has happened. The
Swedes had attacked the castle; Ronald came as a messenger of peace,
but was misunderstood. In the ensuing fight, he was killed together
with the girls' father and their brother. Clarissa and Johanna remain
unmarried and live to be very old. Gregor keeps his promise, burns
the house at the lake and plants seeds of trees on the spot. People
see him wander through the woods like a phantom, but they cannot
tell when they have seen him last.

Der Hochwald is, no doubt, in many respects still indebted to
Romantic tradition, especially in the way nature is pictured: as a
living being, listening, seeing, feeling, and marveling at the first
sight of human beings. Romantic are the fairy-tale prince Ronald,
the exalted Clarissa, the melancholy knight Bruno, and the almost
mythical character of Gregor. Equally Romantic are the mysterious
Wildschütz and his bullet, the use of folklore and folksong. But
everything mysterious and seemingly supernatural has its rational
explanation and is not an integral part of the story as it is, for example,
in Tieck's *Der blonde Eckbert*. Besides, the descriptions of the
grandeur, beauty, and peace of the forest are more forceful and
realistic than any written by a Romantic writer. They are written
by a man who had lived and intimately communed with nature, seen
it with the keenly observant eye of a painter, and had the gift of
words even more than that of the brush. The technique is that of an
impressionistic, *plein-air* painter, an interplay of lights, shadows,
and colors. There is a rapport between nature and man, a mystical
union, probably never reached before or after Stifter.

What unites *Der Hochwald* with all of Stifter's work, besides
this intimate rapport with nature, is his pacifist attitude. Although

the story takes place during one of the bloodiest wars of history, the description of fighting occupies only two pages. Already in *Feld-blumen* Stifter had said, *"noch sind Kriege"* (there are still wars, I, 56). In *Der Hochwald,* he contrasts the slow effort and care with which the forest nurtures the smallest of its flowers with the haste and frivolity with which man destroys the most precious and marvelous plant, that is, himself. Johanna rails against false hero worship in a passage which foreshadows similar words in *Die Mappe,* the Preface to *Bunte Steine, Bergmilch,* and *Witiko.*[15]

Another tie with the whole of Stifter's work is the emphasis on kindness and innocence, in which youth (the two sisters) and old age (their father and Gregor) share. Even Ronald, who has roamed through the wide world, has remained "candid," "gentle," "innocent" (287). The guileless Johanna, higher in the scale of value than the man who has conquered evil in himself, reminds Stifter of Jesus' warning: "Woe unto him who offends one of these little ones!"—one of the few places where Stifter refers to Jesus (220). There are no villains in the story. The relations between father and daughters and between the two sisters are delicate, tender, and loving. The sisters are very close to each other, and Stifter shows less reserve in depicting outward signs of affection than he does in later stories. There is even a certain sensuousness in their love. Clarissa had been both mother and example for the younger Johanna, and this imposes some restraint on the passionate love scene between Ronald and Clarissa. However, it still impresses the modern reader as rather melodramatic, abounding in superlatives, which Stifter, in his later style, uses very sparingly or altogether avoids. Lunding sees in the Ronald scenes a regression to the style of *Feldblumen.*

Much was made, at the beginning of serious Stifter research, of the influence of James Fenimore Cooper's Leatherstocking Tales, especially *The Deerslayer,* on *Der Hochwald.*[16] Modern scholars tend to see no more than a possible stimulus, a view with which this author agrees. It cannot be denied that there are similarities of plot between the two stories: seeking protection on or at a lake in troubled times, a father taking care of two motherless daughters, and some minor details. But the most striking similarity— the pantheism, the idea that "the whole earth is a temple of the Lord," a book in which those who cannot read the printed word can see God's handwriting, His unending bounty and goodness—

all this rests on affinity between the two writers rather than on influence.[17] Love of nature, untouched and unspoiled by human hands, was fundamental to both men. It is interesting to note that, at the end of both stories, human abodes disappear, and the solitude of nature is restored. As far as the characters are concerned, parallels drawn between the two pairs of sisters, Clarissa and Johanna, and Judith and Hetty Hutter, are untenable. Of the male characters, only the Deerslayer could have inspired Stifter, through his kindness and deep love of nature, his reverence for life as shown in his dealings with the Indians, and his bitter regret for having shot an eagle out of sheer vanity.[18] The two other principal male characters, Tom Hutter (the father) and Harry Hurry, crude, brutal, scalp-hunting for profit, are as un-Stifterian as possible. So are the strong suspense, sustained throughout most of Cooper's novel, the many gruesome scenes, and, last but not least, the "realistic" dialogues, making use of the ungrammatical speech of frontier man.

Die Narrenburg (Fools' Castle), the second story of Volume II of the *Studien,* is, together with the first version of *Die Mappe* and *Prokopus,* one of the so-called Scharnast stories. It is safe to assume that Stifter had originally planned them as a unit, the chronicle of the counts of Scharnast, of which only fragments were actually written.[19] Count Hanns von Scharnast had, long ago, established a strange condition of inheritance: the heir to the Rothenstein may take possession only if he swears to write down truthfully the history of his life up to his death, to be deposited in a special vault, and to read all the memoirs deposited before his time. Hanns had made this stipulation so that each heir could learn from his predecessors and so that the fear of being forced to record his follies for posterity would prevent him from committing them. But Hanns's good intentions had the opposite result. Soon people were calling the Rothenstein Fools' Castle, and the motto of the story reads: "Behold, what sinister tales these ruins tell."

A family curse is, no doubt, a Romantic theme, but Stifter's denouement, as we shall see, is quite un-Romantic. The basic themes of the story—the importance of the family *(Geschlecht),* the question of heredity, the puzzling phenomenon that each being is an individual and, at the same time, only a link in an endless chain of generations—occur again and again in Stifter's work. Like any sensitive poet, Stifter felt strongly the vanity and transitoriness of human existence; he understood the desire to perpetuate one's individual self in children, possessions, buildings, memoirs, and portraits. But he also knew the futility of this desire. In the only memoirs included in the story, those of Jodok, we read that every life is new and unique. Everyone believes that he is the keystone of all that went before, that he is the center of the universe. Yet everything passes away, we know not whither.[20] According to Jodok, nothing that remains of an individual matters after the "I" *(Ich)* is gone, "the sweet, beautiful miracle which never returns" (I, 414). Whatever the "I" leaves behind should be consigned to the pure, golden, consuming fire. Only the air he breathed should remain because it continues as fresh as for the millions who breathed it before him. These are strange words for an author who believes in the immortality of the individual soul. Those puzzling questions for which there is really no answer well up again and again in Stifter. It is as if he had forbidden himself to dwell on them and thus become aware of any contradictions to his religious beliefs.

The chronicle of the Scharnast family is related in stories within a story. The framework is life at the inn *zur grünen Fichtau,* at a spot where the valley is wide enough for the inn, a sawmill, a smithy, and a few houses. Stifter calls the story "a dusky, gloomy picture in a bright friendly frame" (363). In the first and last chapters, he uses the same words to describe the splendor and peace of this remote valley in the evening.[21] On Saturday nights, people like to gather at the inn after a week of hard and often dangerous work. As later on in *Die Mappe, Der Waldsteig, Der beschriebene Tännling,* and *Witiko,* Stifter expresses his deep affection for the robust, simple, but kind and gay mountain people of his homeland, especially the woodcutters, "the most wonderful young men in the world." Nobody is in a hurry at the inn, and Stifter's leisurely style conveys this mood.[22] Among the guests of the Fichtau one evening is a young naturalist, Heinrich, who from conversations with other people learns a great deal about the Fools' Castle, the ruins of which he had discovered that very afternoon without being able to find the entrance. He hears about the quarrel of the two hostile brothers, Julianus and Julius. Julianus, one of the few villains in Stifter's work, robbed his brother of his maternal inheritance. Julius went away and was never seen again. From what Heinrich hears at the inn and from what he has heard at home, he suspects that he is a descendant of Julius and the heir to the Rothenstein.

After night has descended on the Fichtau, Heinrich and Anna, the innkeeper's daughter, meet secretly in the garden. Anna is a lovely, innocent child of nature, who follows her heart—a *Biedermeier* version of Goethe's Gretchen. Fortunately for her, Heinrich is no Faust, although he praises her innocence and humility in words very similar to those of Faust. The restraint of her family upbringing also weighs more heavily on Anna than on Gretchen: she will not meet Heinrich in a second tryst. A seduction scene, after all, is unthinkable in Stifter's work.

Together with his friend, the town clerk, Heinrich visits Fools' Castle, where Stifter's imagination runs riot. Within the iron wall which circles the mountain like a black diadem, they find an enormous variety of buildings and gardens, all in a lesser or greater state of decay. Wherever possible, nature has taken over: in every little crack, grass and flowers sprout; shimmering lizards run over the sphinxes in a courtyard; in some former cloisters, bees have built honeycombs. Although Stifter is not immune to the Romantic charm of such a wilderness, the general disarray, the destruction, the dirt and dust, hurt his sense of order and beauty.[23] The only people still living on the mountain are the former castellan Ruprecht, his granddaughter Pia, and an old woman servant. Pia is a beautiful child, but wild and shy, the first representative in Stifter's work of Mignon's family. Ruprecht's mind is confused; his mysterious and disjointed remarks are of little help to Heinrich and his friend. Finally they enter the magnificent green hall, so called because of its green serpentine walls. It contains the portraits of all the Scharnasts, and in one of them Heinrich discovers a striking likeness to himself. It is, therefore, no great surprise when he turns out to be a descendant of the Scharnast family and heir to the Rothenstein. A letter from his mother furnishes the necessary proof. Heinrich deposits his life story in the vault and reads one memoir, the tragic story of Jodok and Chelion, a short *Novelle* by itself. Blackall calls it "a most powerful piece of passionate, sensual writing."[24] Chelion is a beautiful pariah girl whom Jodok brings from the Indian Himalayas to be his wife. But one cannot transplant such delicate flowers; she languishes in the northern climate. In her innocence she falls victim to her brother-in-law's passion and responds, for a fleeting moment, to his arduous embrace. Jodok plans to kill her but, like all of Stifter's heroes, does not go through with his criminal plans. Chelion, however, having read the intent in his eyes, cannot regain her confidence in him, without which she cannot live. She wastes away and dies. Many years after her death, Jodok, old and alone, sets fire to the building which had been their home.

Die Narrenburg closes with the marriage of Heinrich and Anna. The Rothenstein and the Fichtau, which throughout the whole story, are used contrapuntally—the one a symbol of confusion and misery, the other of peace—are now united in harmony, and peace and order will be restored on the Rothenstein too. Heinrich has everything cleaned and all the buildings repaired, first seeing to it that everything should be beautiful and gracious. Later on the "useful and lasting" aspect will slowly be developed. What could be less Romantic! Unceasing activity and creativity *(ein restloses Wirken und Schaffen)* begin with Heinrich's reign. He succeeds where Jodok has failed: he raises innocent Anna, whom he compares to Chelion, to his level. She becomes a *hohe Frau,* who bears him two healthy sons, who, we can assume, will not leave their father, as did Count Christoph. Heinrich takes care of old Ruprecht and adopts Pia, who grows up to be a beautiful maiden, pure and gentle as an angel—altogether "a happy ending to the sad stories of the Rothenstein."

It is easy to see that *Die Narrenburg* lacks artistic unity. It is still worth reading, however, because it contains so many descriptive passages of exquisite beauty and many ideas to be developed more fully in later works.

Prokopus, which appeared in the magazine *Iris* four years after the *Studien* version of *Die Narrenburg,* but was never included in the *Studien,* leads us back once more to the troubled past of the Scharnasts. It is the story of the unhappy marriage of Prokopus and Gertraud, parents of the hostile brothers Julianus and Julius. Of Prokopus himself we learn very little in *Die Narrenburg.* We see the half-poetic, half-insane glance on his portrait; we learn that he was an astrologer who had a high Gothic tower built for his studies and then had cords strung from its top to its bottom, a kind of huge Aeolian harp. When the wind carries the sound to the woodcutters on the mountains, they believe that the ghost of Prokopus is haunting the castle.

In the present story, we meet him as an extremely handsome young man of great promise leading his bride to his paternal castle. The procession passes through the valley of the Fichtau, and all have a morning meal at the inn which we know so well from *Die Narrenburg*. Almost half of *Prokopus* deals with life at the inn, because, as Stifter says here, as well as in *Die Narrenburg,* he had a weakness for this "unpretentious," but free and happy life. The meal which the distinguished guests consume at the inn is described with the ceremoniousness so characteristic of Stifter's later style. But the innkeeper seems almost glad to see them depart. Now he can have everything cleaned, put away, and arranged in the accustomed order. In typical Stifterian fashion, even the horses' troughs have to be scrubbed, because the foreign horses might have had some disease!

The couple and their guests proceed to the castle to perform a second wedding ceremony. There are many ominous signs: some of the festive garlands at the gate have fallen down; the welcoming cheers of the crowd resemble a stormy roar; the church is dark, and the statues of the saints look down upon them almost menacingly. At night, when the lovely surroundings cannot be seen, the couple steps out onto a balcony and the bride has a terrible sensation of floating in the air. A shooting star crosses the sky, but Prokopus refuses to accept it as an ill omen; he will take it only as a symbol of how rapidly time will pass for them in their happiness. But happiness never comes; their characters are too different. Gertraud's nature is deep and quiet; she loves clarity and harmony, and the Rothenstein remains uncanny for her. Her world is limited; she is afraid of everything she cannot assimilate: hence her hostility toward Bernard von Kluen, her husband's friend and former tutor, an extraordinary person and scholar. Prokopus is the very opposite: he is open and gay. His mind, like that of his ancestors, is keen, aggressive, reaching into the unknown, restless and enterprising. Prokopus and Gertraud love each other with a deep passion and yet hurt each other "as with sharp knives" (III, 553).

Things are quite different in the Fichtau, as contrasted with the castle. Romanus and Ludmilla, the innkeeper and his wife, live to a very old age in undiminished love and harmony, and they have no unworthy son like Count Julianus. Romanus's descendants inherit the family's longevity and, as the last sentence of the story reports, joy and prosperity dwell in this house.

Not wholly unjustly, criticism has been leveled at the imbalance of the three chapters, "Am Morgen," "Am Mittag," "Am Abend," the first being so much longer than the second and, especially, the third. The increasing, irreparable estrangement between husband and wife is only sketched, masterly as the strokes may be. Although Prokopus and Gertraud are not portraits of Stifter and Amalia, the conflicts in the two marriages in some ways seem to resemble each other.

Die Mappe meines Urgrossvaters (The Memoirs of my Great-grandfather) occupies a central place in the *Studien* and in Stifter's work in general. It is the only *Studie* which fills a volume by itself (Vol. III) and the only work which accompanied Stifter through almost all of his literary life. He called it his "favorite child," an "especially beautiful part of his soul."[25] Comprising all the essential elements of his art, it contains one of his most famous nature descriptions, is rooted in his native countryside, its traditions and people, and is steeped in his love of old things. Much of the story is devoted to describing the joy of planting and building, of creating and caring for things *(das Richten und Schaffen),* in many ways a prelude to *Der Nachsommer.* Most important, however, is the fact that Stifter's specific ethos is here developed fully for the first time. Individual happiness, as far as it is based on relationships with other human beings, is not always in our power. We may lose our beloved through death or through our own fault; yet there is another happiness which stems from sublimating our grief, from becoming good and gentle, from doing our duty faithfully and indefatigably, thus helping our fellow men. This truth, when stated theoretically, sounds banal enough, like almost every great truth, but when exemplified in the lives of the two main characters, the colonel and the doctor, it becomes deeply moving and convincing. It is, as has often been noted, also the essence of Goethe's Weltanschauung, especially in his *Wilhelm Meister.*

The organization of the story is rather complex: there are really two stories contained within a frame. The first and last chapters, an introduction and conclusion, narrated by the author, form the framework. During a visit to his home, he finds the *Mappe,* that is, the notebook containing the memoirs of his great-grandfather, the doctor Augustinus. The memoirs contain not only the story of the doctor's life and of his love for Margarita, the colonel's daughter, but also the story of the colonel's life, complete in itself.

The first chapter, "Die Altertümer" (The Antiques), largely autobiographical, is devoted to the "poetry of old, worthless things, that melancholy gentle poetry." As a boy, Stifter had been attracted to these objects by their colorfulness, their strangeness, and their mystery. They were to him an old picturebook, for which only the grandfather knew the explanation, and it hurt the boy when one of them was destroyed. These antiques now speak to the mature artist, asking him, as it were, to tell their story. They are the mute tokens of bygone lives, of baptisms, weddings, funerals. Insignificant happenings perhaps, but for Stifter, this history of family life, with its immeasurable wealth of human love and pain, is more important than world history, where love is omitted and only bloodshed is recorded. Love, says Stifter, is the rule, and hatred the exception. Old things fade, tear, go out of fashion, become worthless and are finally thrown away by one's grandsons and replaced by new, not always more beautiful things. But the old things are our link to the past. Whenever we see small children playing beside them, we become aware that we are only links in the chain of generations, but we feel less lonely and isolated in this consciousness of continuity. We know that it is futile to try to prolong this "sweet life" beyond the grave (as we have seen in *Die Narrenburg*), yet we bequeath our possessions to our descendants, who look with melancholy at these last shadowy traces of their ancestors and see their own shadows follow them in the future. This chapter of *Die Mappe,* as well as the essay "Der Tandelmarkt" (The Flea Market), is an elegy on the transient nature of all earthly things, whereas "Ein Gang durch die Katakomben," a grim variation on the same theme, fills us with horror.[26]

In essence, the great-grandfather's story is rather simple. As a young doctor, Augustinus comes back from the University of Prague and begins to practice in his native woods, where there had never before been a doctor. His father, a simple farmer, and his two sisters love and admire him and help him in every possible way. But all three die. Their little cottage is distasteful to Augustinus now, and he moves into the larger house he had started to build before their death. After a hard winter, in which a heavy ice storm occurs, he meets his new neighbors, the colonel and his daughter Margarita. A real friendship ensues, the younger man learning from the older.

This socratic relationship is a frequent and important motif in Stifter's work. Augustinus shares with Margarita his intimate knowledge of nature, and her willingness to learn reveals her growing love for him. Finally, the young people confess their mutual love. As in *Feldblumen,* an unjustified, though understandable, fit of jealousy destroys everything. The scene in the Lidenholz, where Augustinus sees his beloved in an intimate conversation with her cousin, is a repetition of the scene in the park of Schönbrunn. Margarita then tells the doctor that she cannot marry a man who does not trust her fully and questions her former avowal of love. The girl, in all her gentleness, has that unbending quality so characteristic of many of Stifter's heroines and so often overlooked by the critics. The doctor, unable to change her decision, wants to commit suicide. The colonel, afraid of what Augustinus may do in his despair, follows him into the woods, but without letting him know why he has come. He hints at our insignificance in the general order of things by pointing out how beautifully the grain is growing this year. The colonel's brief presence, without any discussion of Augustinus' intent—a subtle omission—makes it impossible for the doctor to go through with his sinister plan after the colonel has left. Two days later, the colonel tells him his life story, how from a gambler and brawler he has become *"der sanftmütige Obrist"* (gentle colonel), as he is called. Most important in accomplishing this change have been: first, the advice of a comrade-in-arms to record his experiences and thoughts and not to reread these memoirs until at least three years have past; then, grief at the sudden loss of his young wife. The need to examine his actions and feelings retrospectively changed his moral outlook, and in the midst of war and bloodshed he became a gentler human being *(ein sanfterer Mensch).* Looking back on his life, he thinks that his greatest deed was to have saved, through negotiations, at the risk of his own life, the lives of a thousand enemies.

Augustinus adopts the idea of the memoirs as a means of maturing through continuous self-examination, and thus the *Mappe* comes into being. The idea is more successful than in *Die Narrenburg,* because it is a question of reading one's own, and not other people's memoirs. Augustinus also sublimates his grief over the loss of Margarita, and his great loneliness, into an ever greater dedication to his patients. Thus, he finds himself again, and with himself, the outer world—for Stifter one and the same thing. In his fit of jealousy, Augustinus had decapitated the flowers he had intended to take to Margarita, a wanton act of destruction which prepares the reader for the later idea of suicide. Completely oblivious to "everything in heaven and earth," he had wanted to "tear up, destroy, *punish* the things of this world";[27] now in saving, single-handed, an innocent youth by means of an extremely dangerous operation, he feels that he has regained "the trees, woods, heaven and earth" (I, 640). This is Stifter's special way of saying that everything pales beside the thought of having done one's duty. Margarita, after three years' absence, cannot but realize what an admirable man *(herrlicher Mann)* Augustinus has become and is willing to be his wife. The reunion takes place at a popular shooting match, the colorful description of which gives Stifter ample opportunity to revel in memories of his youth.

Actually, in the above *Studien* version Stifter does not follow the chronological order of our summary.[28] His sequence is: the vow of the doctor to start his memoirs, a short hint at the unsuccessful wooing of Margarita, the intent to commit suicide, the colonel's story, then the young doctor's beginnings to the time of his separation from Margarita. Although the chapter following the colonel's story is called "Margarita," it is only after more than seventy pages of narrative that we meet her for the first time. Stifter's delight in describing man's creative activity in caring for his surroundings carried him beyond the limits of a *Novelle*. When reading the proofs, he was dissatisfied with his achievement, even more than was habitual with him. With honesty amazing in a letter to one's publisher, he disparaged his own work. He had aimed at the highest goal: to reveal greatness of character through ordinary events and circumstances. Now he found his work uneven, considering the best part to be the narration and the character of the colonel.[29] This story within the main story is, as not infrequently happens with Stifter, a piece of extremely compact writing without descriptive digressions. While revising the first version for the *Studien,* Stifter had called it "of granite," "classical," and with it he believed he had refuted a critic who had denied him the faculty of concise writing (*Br I,* 132 f.). There is no more dramatic scene in Stifter's work than the death of the colonel's young wife. She falls into an abyss, overcome by an attack of dizziness while crossing a narrow bridge without railings. Nowhere has Stifter conveyed to us so strongly the incomprehensibility of such a sudden death and the utter indifference of nature, in whose household such a loss is no more than that of a tiny golden fly (496). The lonely vigil of the husband beside the body of his wife *is* of classical simplicity. It is as poetic as it is sad: the reflections of the red evening clouds softly fill the room with roses.

Another high point in *Die Mappe* is the description of the ice storm. The doctor and his servant must go out, and the reader, following them step by step, vicariously experiences their feelings of admiration and fear. What is perhaps unparalleled in literature is the sober exactitude with which Stifter describes the storm without losing anything of its grandeur. He never deals in generalities: a frozen bush looks to him like many candles twisted together, or like luminous, watery, shining corals; his wooden fence recalls the silver gate before the altar. Here, the term "poetic realism," so often misused, is quite appropriate. The following spring repairs the damage caused by the storm; it even looks as if the trees had benefited from their wounds. This is probably an unrealistic, overly optimistic view, as Stifter must have known himself. Some lives are lost in the ice storm, but nothing happens to any of the people whom the reader knows. The same good fortune prevails in the doctor's work: his patients recover or at least improve. It is true that his nearest relatives die, but one sentence laconically reports his vain efforts to help them; and in the last version of the story (1867), they are carried off by an epidemic, where even a skilled physician is helpless. Rather ugly-looking wounds and tumors are briefly described, but we are spared any description of insufferable pain or death agony. We may be thankful for such omissions and at the same time feel dissatisfied with Stifter's limitations as a man and artist. One has only to read Camus' account of the cruel suffering of a child in *La Peste* and Dr. Rieux's words to the priest, *"Et je refuserai jusqu'à la mort d'aimer cette création où des enfants sont torturés,"* to understand how completely Stifter evades the ultimate theological question—the suffering of innocent creatures.

CHAPTER 3

Studien: *Volumes IV to VI*

HAD Stifter written only the stories discussed so far, he probably would have gone down in the history of literature simply as a *Heimatdichter* (regional poet) who could excel only in descriptions of familiar landscapes and people. In the last three volumes of the *Studien*, however, his imagination extends to regions he had never seen: the African desert in *Abdias*, the Hungarian *puszta* in *Brigitta*, and a high plateau above Lake Garda in *Zwei Schwestern*.

Abdias, which won its author great fame at its first publication in 1843, differs from the other *Studien* in being more dramatic (especially in the much shorter first version) and less reserved in depicting violent scenes and emotions. With uncanny empathy Stifter succeeds in evoking vivid pictures of the African desert and of the life of an ethnic group completely alien to him, that of the African Jews. His picture of the Jews in *Abdias* is remarkably objective: he sees their bad as well as their good sides. They are cunning, hard, unrelenting bargainers, laying almost exclusive emphasis on material goods. But Stifter is very careful to show that it is really the hostile, unjust, and merciless Gentile world which forces them into such a position.[1] Side by side with this materialism, there is, in the main characters, a vague spiritual longing which they cannot satisfy because they do not know how. Their virtues are their tenacity, their patience and endurance, and their close family life. Great love within the family must compensate for the scorn and suffering endured in the outside world. Abdias follows to the letter the biblical command: "Thou shalt honor thy father and mother."

Abdias could almost be called a short novel, since it spans three generations and takes the hero from the cradle to the grave.[2] A summary cannot give more than the bare outline. The story is set in the deserts of the Atlas region, in the ruins of a Roman town inhabited now only by some Jews and jackals. Hidden deep within these squalid ruins, Abdias's father Aron has sumptuously furnished rooms for his wife Esther and her servants. Abdias is their only child, pampered by his mother, but sent out early into the world by his father in order to learn the art of commerce, the only means of survival for a Jew. He leaves his home an affectionate, handsome youth. But the Gentiles treat him as if he were an unfeeling thing, to be hurt with impunity. Thus, he becomes hard, unrelenting, and spiteful in his dealings with them and devotes his love and loyalty to his camel. After fifteen years he returns a rich man, and a feast like that described in the parable of the Prodigal Son is celebrated. Soon after the feast he leaves again for Balbek to fetch his bride, the beautiful Deborah. His parents die, he gets richer and richer, sharing his wealth with his animals, slaves, and neighbors. The latter hate him for it, since he is superior and different (*Urf.,* p. 15). He loses his great beauty through smallpox, and with his beauty, Deborah's love.

Abdias tries to compensate for his unhappiness at home by winning esteem and power in the outside world, although he suspects that he owes them only to his wealth. But he goes too far. He offends Melek, the emissary of the Bey, by making him wait a long time before granting his request for a loan. This arrogance, although very understandable after all the humiliations he has suffered, brings on his downfall. He has still one great moment as the leader in a battle between his caravan and some attacking Bedouins. Thoughts of killing the Bey, of becoming Bey, of becoming Sultan, and of conquering the whole world assail him on his lonely ride home. But just the opposite happens: he loses his most precious possessions, his wife, and his home. During Abdias's absence, Melek, with some mercenaries, has sacked the desert town. Exasperated by Melek's taunts, Abdias, on his return, tries to shoot him, fails and is mercilessly beaten by Melek's soldiers. But Deborah has borne him a little girl, and "in the midst of destruction he felt as if the greatest happiness on earth had come to him" (II, 29). He himself is reborn, and this happiness radiating from within makes him beautiful again for Deborah. Husband and wife, who have both now lost their physical beauty, are reunited in a deeper union than ever—but only for a fleeting moment.[3] Abdias must leave to find nourishment for mother and child, and while he is away, Deborah, in her inexperience, bleeds to death. Abdias's discovery of her death, his caring for the newborn babe, the picture of his long shadow falling across the body of his wife, the burial—all this has the classic grandeur and simplicity for which Stifter was always striving. Only two of Abdias's servants return, his Abyssinian slave Uram, who loves him, and Deborah's favorite servant Mirtha, who hates him but wants to take care of Ditha, the little girl.

With great prudence (and Stifter's love for details) Abdias now prepares for their emigration. He takes leave of the desert as if it were paradise (57). Uram is left behind but, risking his life, follows them on a camel and reaches them after two days, completely exhausted.[4] Mirtha remains in Africa; only Uram accompanies his master to Europe and dies there during the first year in the northern climate. Thus, Abdias finds himself alone in the isolated valley which he chooses for his new home. With the complete absorption characteristic of all his actions, Abdias now devotes himself to the education of Ditha, only to discover that the poor child is blind. He becomes obsessed with the thought that once more in his life, he will have to amass wealth so that she will be protected after his death. Then, when she is eleven years old, lightning strikes her room and gives her sight. Through Ditha's love and perfect companionship, Abdias now experiences the few happy years he is ever to know. With infinite patience he introduces her into the world of the seeing; he is the only one who understands her, in whom, because of her long blindness, sounds and colors, dream and reality mingle, whereas to others she is as strange as if she were a "talking flower" (102). Like Schiller's Polycrates, Abdias is afraid of this excess of happiness and wants to appease fate by sacrificing something dear to him. But to no avail. Lightning, which has given Ditha her sight, strikes and kills her while father and daughter sit watching a thunderstorm in a little house made of sheaves. This happens at the very moment when she speaks of the shrouds that her beloved linen furnishes for the dead. Her death leaves Abdias in a stupor. When, after years, he comes out of it, he wants to go to Africa to take revenge on Melek. But now he is too feeble. He lives to a very old age—according to some, more than a hundred years.

The unity of this long story is maintained by the tall, dominating figure of Abdias, who, in one scene after another, comes before our eyes as clearly as in a sequence of shots in a film. Among the most striking pictures we find: the youth on his camel, with his burning eyes looking out into the wastes of the desert, musing, as beautiful as one of the divine messengers who had come to his people (15); the virile, impassioned leader in the frenzy of battle, depicted as in a canvas by Delacroix (22f.); the suffering, but still undaunted man, silent, footsore, walking through the desert in front of the she-ass that carries his child and the hostile servant

(60); the "haggard, ugly Jew" crossing the gangplank, clasping the child to his bosom instead of bundles of goods, followed by Uram, a beautiful dark bronze statue, so to speak, and the half-starved she-ass (71); the white-haired man, his dark face marred by old age and pockmarks, beside his slender, fair daughter (99); the father, striding in the wind, carrying his dead child on his shoulder, her head and arm dangling on his back (113).

The unity of the story also lies in the local color of the African desert which Stifter carries over into the European scenes, "the gray of the desert and of far distances" (71). Abdias chooses a lonely valley for his new home, because its quiet barrenness reminds him of the "loveliness" of the desert. He builds and furnishes his house in a way more suited to the climate of the desert than to that of an Austrian mountain valley. He never loses his joy in the miraculous abundance of fresh, cool water. He continues to wear his African clothes, whereas Ditha's are a compromise between the African and European styles. He likes to speak Arabic with Ditha, tells her tales of the desert, and "throws his Bedouin thoughts like an Atlas vulture against her heart" when he wants to talk seriously (verständig) with her so as to develop her reasoning power (107)! He never tempers the violence of his emotions, as shown in the excessive grief over the loss of his dog (brought about through his own fault)[5] and his continuing desire to revenge himself on Melek (74, 114). Both father and daughter love to sit in the hot noonday sun when everybody else is seeking shelter. Ditha is compared to the slender shaft of a desert aloe growing beside alder and juniper bushes. They remain alone, "and the sun that shone on the valley was, as it were, a bleak African sun" (106).

The question has been raised whether Abdias's fate is typical of the general human condition or whether Stifter intended it to be predominantly Jewish.[6] The sequence of hiding, persecution, migration, and alienation in the new homeland is certainly characteristic of the Jewish destiny. But beneath the Jewishness of Abdias lies a universal core, and in the interweaving of both lies Stifter's art. Abdias is an African Jew, fashioned by his upbringing and his ethnic fate, but he is also universal man with an infinite capacity for action, hatred, love, grief and joy. None of the spiritually significant events of his life have anything to do with his being a Jew.

The chief difficulty for the interpreter of *Abdias* has always been the philosophical introduction, where Stifter wrestles with the problem of the apparent irrationality (modern existentialists would say absurdity) of human destiny, the problem of the relation of fate and human responsibility *(Schicksal und Schuld)*, which underlies much of his writing. He is deeply troubled by the "placid innocence" with which the laws of nature operate, and the "engaging counten-ance" with which she dispenses her gifts, bliss or disaster. He ponders over the difference between the concept of *"fatum"* in the ancient world (the "terrible, final, immovable cause of all happen-ing, . . . the ultimate irrationality of Being") and the less stringent modern concept of *"Schicksal"* (fate) which presupposes a higher power as a sender (the German word *"schicken"* means to send). But even the latter concept offers no explanation for the sudden disasters which befall man, and Stifter tries to get out of this difficulty by seeing human destiny as a "bright garland of flowers," the chain of causes and effects, whose end lies in the hand of God. One day, he would have us believe, our reason will see all the links of the chain and recognize that every misfortune is caused by our own wrongdoing. But, as Walter Silz rightly says, Abdias's "career disproves at every turn" this "facile optimism." "Optimism about life may be Stifter's wish, but pessimism is his conviction."[7]

Stifter himself must have been dissatisfied with his solution of the problem, for he closes his introduction with the remark that destinies like that of Abdias make one ask "Why must it be so?" and lure one into "a gloomy brooding about Providence, Destiny and the ultimate basis of all things." Various attempts by Stifter scholars to exonerate fate by making Abdias responsible for his misfortunes seem uncon-vincing to me.[8] His faults are more than balanced by his good qualities; his upbringing and treatment at the hands of others account in large part for his "wrongdoings." The neighbors who see God's punishments in his misfortunes judge from what they superficially observe, without possessing real insight. Even if we could accept the idea of "punishment," it still would be out of proportion to his "crime." Stifter himself never judges Abdias and asks the reader who may have heard of him or seen him as an old man not to harbor any "bitter feeling" against him, but to withhold judgment until he has read the story.

Even if we find fault with the author's metaphysical introduction, we cannot but admire the story itself, which is deeply moving. Its poetry, the brilliance of its style—the glowing, exotic colors, the luxuriance of pictorial imagination, the felicity of its metaphors—are unsurpassed in Stifter's work. Thomas Mann felt that no modern writer, not even a Kasimir Edschmid, measured up to Stifter's art.[9] *Abdias* will remain one of the most widely read of Stifter's stories. It has recently been included, in a new translation, in an English anthology of German narrative prose.[10]

The next, less familiar part of *Studien, Das alte Siegel* (The Ancient Seal), is remarkable in showing that the moralist Stifter was no narrow-minded puritan. In the conflict between honor and humanity, he clearly sides with the latter. Veit Hugo Evaristus Almot grows up a motherless boy in a remote mountain village under the sole tutelage of his old father, a former soldier. The father is the epitome of uprightness and honesty, but rather limited in his human experience. Fixation on his father determines much of Hugo's later fate.[11] At the age of twenty-one, a handsome, chaste young man, he goes to the capital to finish his education and prepare himself for the expected uprising against Napoleon. Like so many of Stifter's youths, he follows his course with singleness of purpose. His father dies and leaves him, besides a small estate, the family seal: *servandus tantummodo honos* (Honor must be preserved above all).

A mysterious letter from an old man, asking him to come at a certain time to St. Peter's Church, is the turning point in his life. He meets his fate in the person of a young woman who comes there every day, hiding her beauty under a heavy veil and unshapely black clothes. By accident he sees her with her veil lifted. A slow, strange courtship follows. She finally allows him to visit her in a little suburban house, on the one condition, however, that he will not ask anything about her person or circumstances—the Lohengrin motif with roles reversed. All he knows of her is her name, Cöleste. A summer of happiness ensues, clouded by frequent sadness on Cöleste's part and by the uncanny, "unlived-in" atmosphere of the little house. Once when Hugo goes home late on a stormy night, the thought flashes through his mind that their love is not the "pure" love of which he has dreamt all his youth.

At this moment of crisis, the song of a caged finch recalls his old mountain home, the cheery song of the birds there, and he imagines his gray-haired *innocent* father standing in front of the house (162).[12]

He does not visit Cöleste for three days; on the fourth day he returns to find the little house empty, and his elaborate search for her is futile. It is only after eleven years, at the end of the Wars of Liberation, that he finds her again, in a castle in France. What happened to Hugo in the war is omitted because it has no direct bearing upon the story or because of Stifter's aversion to depicting "those heroic deeds which rend the human heart," "the sinister aspects of the human race" (168). The importance of Hugo's participation in the war is that he has become rather firm, severe, and cold for his age. His once handsome, good-natured features show some harshness, and his eyes have grown stern. What has not changed is his strong sense of justice and honor.

Cöleste can now solve all the mysteries for him. She was an orphan. Her guardian had married her, at the age of fifteen, to a French aristocrat, a man of fifty. They had to flee France. When the marriage remained childless, her husband mistreated her. It was then that she vowed to go to church every day veiled and disguised as an old woman, to implore the Virgin to take from her the curse of childlessness. Her husband had to go back to France on a secret mission. The rest was the work of her devoted steward Dionys, who wanted to end Cöleste's misery by substituting another man's child as heir. She herself had been no accomplice to this plan. Stifter stresses the basic purity and innocence of her being. Her name Cöleste may be symbolic of this fact.[13]

Cöleste's husband has been dead for many years, and she has every right to hope for a belated happy union. But Hugo cannot forgive her for deceiving him and her husband. Cöleste asks him whether he could really sacrifice the true warmth of human life to so-called honor.[14] When he remains silent, she exclaims, "My sin is more human than your virtue," thus summarizing the leading idea of the *Novelle* (179 f.) Not even the sight of the little girl she has borne him can change his decision. This attitude is so inhuman, so utterly egotistical, that Cöleste is forced to conclude that he does not recognize the child as his own.

Hugo goes home and, like many other Stifter heroes, looks after his possessions and helps his neighbors. But unlike those others, he does not find happiness in these activities, because there is no real development in his character. Scruples plague him later, and in his old age, after the harshness of war has worn off, he often bitterly weeps over the loss of Cöleste. He throws the family seal into the crevasse of a nearby glacier which he had liked to visit in his youth, thus symbolizing regret for a life not lived and the sterility of his original concept of honor. He wills his possessions to his daughter, but she lives abroad and cannot come often enough to take care of the estate. The house deteriorates; only the mountains remain in all their splendor. But even they will perish, and maybe, someday, the friendly, beautiful earth itself. And so the story closes on an even more pessimistic note than *Der Hochwald,* the ending of which is similar, but where nature at least is seen as permanent.

There is little description of nature in this *Novelle*; and nature is used only symbolically. It is early morning, spring or summer, when Hugo leaves home, summer when he meets Cöleste, fall when he finds the Lindenhaus empty, and deep winter when he gives up his efforts to find her again. A sky torn by storm clouds reflects his inner turmoil when he realizes that something is wrong with their love. The last meeting between the two lovers takes place at a somber castle in a barren landscape. When Hugo rides back to his division after their final separation, it is a November evening, with a harsh wind blowing, cold blue clouds hiding the landscape, and the dry autumnal grass rustling beside him. One is reminded of Goethe's *Werther,* where the change of the seasons reflects the change of the hero's moods from Book I to Book II.

There has been a great deal of interest lately in *Das alte Siegel,* which used to be considered a minor work. Werner Hoffmann has analyzed the first version in detail; J. P. Stern calls it representative in structure and style of Stifter's finest works; Eric A. Blackall counts it among Stifter's most passionate and strongest creations.[15] Whether or not one agrees with the high rank assigned to the story by these critics, one can gladly subscribe to the renewed interest. The story deserves fresh attention because it is the only one in which Stifter opposes the claims of love and a rigid and unquestioned concept of virtue.

The next *Studie, Brigitta,* ranks with *Abdias* as one of Stifter's best-known stories. It owes its success to mild suspense maintained throughout, the unusual character of the two protagonists, and the superb picture of the *puszta* and its inhabitants.[16] It belongs to the group of works *(Die Mappe, Zwei Schwestern)* which spell out Stifter's message most clearly: man is not to brood in despair over the loss of a beloved person, however the loss occurred. He must dedicate his life to a worthwhile task, which, for Stifter, often means changing hitherto infertile soil into a beautiful piece of productive land. Then he will experience new happiness in what is called in *Brigitta* "the bliss of creating" (II, 238). After thus maturing and winning the respect and love of his neighbors, he may find a new and deeper relationship with his former beloved.

In *Brigitta,* this theme is interwoven with another favorite theme of Stifter's: the possible disparity between physical and spiritual beauty. Angela's twin sister in *Feldblumen,* as well as Hanna in *Der beschrie-bene Tännling,* possess only physical beauty; and Deborah's and Abdias's eyes are opened to spiritual beauty when it is too late. Only Ditha has the gift of seeing inner beauty, perhaps because she had been blind (II, 100). In *Brigitta,* we see the inner strength and beauty of a very plain woman win the enduring love of a very handsome man.

The structure of the story is rather intricate. In the first chapter, "Steppenwanderung," we accompany the narrator through the *puszta,* one of Stifter's vast, melancholy, rather bleak landscapes which have a beauty all their own. Stifter often uses the device of the traveler on foot to acquaint the reader with a certain landscape, so as to avoid a static, boring description. The narrator wants to visit a friend whom he calls "the Major". During his lonely journey, he recalls the character of the latter, whom he had first met in southern Italy, a country almost as solemn and deserted as the *puszta*. The Major was then a man of almost fifty, still extremely handsome and attractive. But what had struck him most was the Major's extreme sensitiveness to beauty. Near Uwar, his friend's estate, the narrator asks his way of a middle-aged woman on horseback, dressed like a man. He takes her for a stewardess and offers her a tip. She declines it, laughing and showing her beautiful teeth. This little episode is one of many subtle ways of arousing our curiosity.[17]

At Uwar we become familiar, in great detail, with a Hungarian estate and with the patriarchal relationship between the owner and his servants and shepherds. They all eat together, and he speaks of them, and addresses them, as his children (210, 213). He also wears the same costume as they do. The guest accompanies his host on his visits to all parts of his vast estate and finally takes on a special responsibility in its administration, thus affirming, in a very Goethean manner, the value and joy of a regular, useful activity. The Major has created a model estate in the midst of the barren *puszta*. To drain a swamp and build a road, he has been able to employ beggars, vagabonds, and even worse (205). In Stifter's world there is no place for good-for-nothings, those popular heroes in nineteenth- and twentieth-century literature.[18]

We learn from Gömör, the Major's friend, whom the narrator visits, that it was not the Major but his neighbor, Brigitta Maroshely, who had created the first model estate in this seemingly infertile country. We also learn from Gömör that Brigitta's husband had left her many years ago and never returned, that the Major had not visited her for several years until she became very ill. Then he came to care for her. From that time on, the two had been close friends, and, as Gömör intimates, the Major had developed an "unnatural" passion for the woman who was so plain and no longer young. When the Major promises his guest a visit to Maroshely, he calls Brigitta the most wonderful woman on this earth. Before this visit the guest also meets her son Gustav, a youth of extraordinary beauty.

The third chapter, "Steppenvergangenheit," relates the story of Brigitta's youth. An ugly child, rejected by her mother as a baby, she had grown into a wild, defiant, lonely young girl of great physical strength, creating for herself a strange inner world. Stifter here anticipates certain aspects of modern child psychology. Brigitta has only one beautiful feature, her large dark eyes. She meets Stephan Murai, a young man of great beauty, who by character and upbringing is peculiarly fitted to recognize her vitality and inner strength and her unlimited, unused capacity for love. The almost unbelievable occurs: she becomes his bride. She is very reluctant at first to accept him, because, as she puts it, being ugly, she can ask only for the highest kind of love, an infinite love, as it were. They marry, and she bears him a son. After a while he begins to take her out a great deal, and she observes that in public he treats her with even more delicate attention than at home and concludes that he has become aware of her lack of beauty. They move to the country. There, on one of his lonely hunts Stephan meets in Gabriele, a neighbor's daughter, the physical beauty so sorely lacking in Brigitta. They meet again, and once, but only once, on an irresistible impulse, he embraces Gabriele. From then on, the two avoid each other. But when by chance they meet again at a party, a deep blush betrays them. Brigitta insists on a divorce. She too (only to a greater extent) possesses that unrelenting, steel-like quality which characterizes so many of the gentler heroines of Stifter. Brigitta and Stephan still love each other, although Stephan says with a voice full of love that he hates her unspeakably. She lets him depart. He leaves her their son, and she goes to the lonely estate, where she resumes her maiden name and creates for herself and her son a new life of far-reaching, ceaseless activity.

The last chapter, "Steppengegenwart," brings as much of a surprise ending as Stifter's unmelodramatic way of storytelling allows. The Major and his guest visit Maroshely quite often, and what Gömör had said is confirmed. There exists a strange relationship between Brigitta and the Major. It is friendship, mutual respect, and sharing of their agricultural endeavors, but underneath it vibrates a tenderness and affection which, in ordinary circumstances, one would call love. On the way back from one of their visits to Maroshely, the Major and his guest find Brigitta's son attacked by a pack of hungry wolves. In one of the most dramatic scenes of Stifter's work—one which belies the common belief that he was incapable of brevity—Gustav is rescued. But he has been wounded, and his mother is called to his sickbed. While she rejoices at his recovery, the Major, asked by his guest why he weeps, simply says, "I have no child." Brigitta, having overheard his words, turns toward the Major, saying nothing but "Stephan." The Major is no other than Stephan Murai, Brigitta's husband. This does not come as a complete surprise, because there have been hints all along. The pattern of *Die Mappe* is repeated in *Brigitta*. The woman who had lost confidence in the man she loves, now sees what he has achieved, how he has gained in moral strength and knows that she can fully trust him.[19]

Love, for Stifter, is inseparable from recognition of the beloved's moral worth. Like Margarita in *Die Mappe*, Brigitta realizes that she has failed too. Brigitta has committed the sin of pride. She and the Major are now able to forgive each other, and with his gift for stating a moral truth in the simplest words, Stifter says, "Noble hearts forgive often—mean ones never" (251). Brigitta and Stephan will never separate again. *"Alles war nun gut"* (All was well now), comments the author, echoing unconsciously the ending of Eichendorff's *Aus dem Leben eines Taugenichts*.[20] The paradox of beauty is resolved: as she forgives, Brigitta's features "radiate inimitable beauty" (250). Earlier in the story Stifter had already indicated how the Major's delicacy of feeling, the respect with which he treated Brigitta, made her appear beautiful.[21] Brigitta is the only heroine in Stifter's work who does not join the procession of women who are as beautiful as they are good (die Schön-Guten), different as they may be in other respects. Therein lies her fascination.

Der Hagestolz (The Old Bachelor), which follows Brigitta, is another famous story in the Studien. Its plot is simple in spite of its length. Victor, an orphan, has been brought up by his foster mother Ludmilla, together with her own daughter Hanna. He has successfully completed his studies, and his guardian has secured him a position in a government office. But before starting work, he must visit his uncle, who lives on a lonely island in a mountain lake and has sent for him. At the request of his uncle, he travels on foot. This, as we have seen in Brigitta, is Stifter's way of acquainting his readers with unknown landscapes: they admire the mountains through the eyes of the awestruck youth, who had never been there. The same device is subsequently used with regard to the island. Victor is virtually a prisoner there and has to amuse himself as best he can by exploring the island in all directions. By and by, uncle and nephew come closer to each other, and, in a flashback, we learn what had happened between the uncle, his brother (Victor's father), and Ludmilla. The uncle had loved Ludmilla, who preferred Victor's father. But the latter did not marry her; out of kindness he married another girl to cover up her father's embezzlement. He never ceased to love Ludmilla and arranged in his will for her to bring up his son. The uncle never loved anybody after he lost Ludmilla; only now, when it is too late, he begins to love Victor. He has secretly saved the father's estate for him and thus enables him to marry Hanna later. Victor resembles his father; Hanna, her mother; thus, in them, the union which their parents had so ardently desired is vicariously consummated.

The plot, when briefly summarized, sounds trivial enough. The art and beauty of the story, however, do not lie in the plot; they lie in the contrapuntal composition and in the description of the landscape, which here has the function of a melody accompanying the main theme. The contrasts are youth and old age, the mother and the bachelor, Victor's home and the uncle's house, the decay of man-made buildings and gardens on the island, and the constant self-renewal of nature.

The first chapter of the story is appropriately called "Gegenbild" (Contrast). The beginning shows us Victor and his friends, noisily enjoying a beautiful spring day's outing. The whole world is still open to them. Their counterpart, introduced at the end of the chapter, is a very old man, afraid of death, sitting alone on a bench in front of his house on an island, the "empty air" and the "futile sunshine" floating around him. He has never married, no old companion now sits beside him, and no child steps into the shadow he casts before him. The house is silent, and there is no one ever to open or close a door for him. The old man is of course Victor's uncle, the bachelor, and the two are again contrasted when they meet later on in the story: the one a haggard old man, wasting away, withdrawn, unkempt; the other a handsome youth, full of vigor and zest for life, innocent, and reflecting, in his cleanliness, the virginal purity of his being. He is one of the many figures in Stifter's work who stand at the threshold between boyhood and manhood. The short-lived radiant bloom and essential purity of this age had a special fascination for Stifter.[22]

Victor is loving, considerate, and trusting; the uncle is self-centered, suspicious, and, at least on the surface, harsh and rude. The contrast between them is brought out sharply in the relationship to their dogs. Victor's dog had rejoined him, in spite of the family's attempt to keep him at home; his young master would rather give up his own life than his dog, as his uncle had demanded of him at first. The uncle has three fat old dogs whom he feeds himself, but nevertheless calls brutes and locks up at night, so that they may not harm him! They soon take to Victor and accompany him gaily on his walks. Rapport with animals is a test of one's full humanity.[23] Victor is good and softhearted, like all of Stifter's youths, but he is more of an individual. He shows youthful traits which the other young people in Stifter's work lack: exaggeration, impatience, infinite desire to do great things, pride, self-assertion, and even defiance. His uncle compares him to a young hawk using his talons.

Victor's youth is contrasted with old age in his uncle and in his foster-mother. Unlike the uncle, she can look back on a life rich in love and care for others; she represents the self-possession, kindness, and serenity which are possible in old age. She herself calls her days now "serene and autumnal" and reprimands Victor for the youthful

exaggeration of his grief (II, 385, 268 f.). But even she experiences
the melancholy of old age, marveling that the years have passed like
a day.[24] Although she has known great grief, she claims that God
grants us only joy and that it is we who add the sorrow. This is
one of Stifter's many tours de force, one of his more or less unconscious distortions of the human condition.

Ludmilla and her home are set in sharp contrast to the uncle and
his surroundings. Her home lies in a friendly hill country with meadows, fields, orchards, and woods. The modest white house lies nestled
among fruit trees and elder bushes. The windows, where snow-white
curtains billow, are always open, whereas the uncle's windows are
always closed and secured by iron bars. The striking of the village
clock, the ringing of the church bell can be heard at her home—sounds
which Victor misses on the island. Signs of life are everywhere: a
friendly dog, chickens, doves, and plants well tended by a gardener
and his small son. Ludmilla takes perfect care of the house—Victor
calls it *"überreinlich"* (overly clean) and her little family. Her world
is small but ordered, a genuine *Biedermeier* world. When we first
meet her, she is dusting and putting things in order. She keeps old,
and now useless, things, like toys, as tokens of a joyous, bygone life,
whereas the uncle has only stuffed birds to dust. Ludmilla's favorite
occupation is bleaching her linen. Stifter considers linen most important for our physical well-being, because it is so close to the body.
Its whiteness symbolizes spiritual purity. In all of Stifter's work, the
uncle is the only person whose linen shirt is soiled, a sign of something
fundamentally wrong in his life. He is a rich man and could very well
afford clean linen. One would rather expect a poor man like the beggar
in the last version of *Die Mappe,* or a man who works with earth like
the gardener in *Der Nachsommer,* to wear soiled linen; yet the clothes
of both are clean.

The uncle's meals are equally symbolic. He is almost a glutton,
but, since his meals are lonely and joyless, he remains haggard, and
his clothes hang loosely on him. The house, too, and the island sym-
bolize his great isolation and loneliness. The lake is surrounded by
well-nigh impassable mountains. The house and the garden are
protected by an impenetrable wall; the gate is always locked. Utter
silence reigns, contrasting sharply with the tumult of lights and
colors on the mountains. The old monastery and once beautiful
gardens are in decay, and the uncle's house is deteriorating. The

uncle and his old servants are the only people on the island. In spite of their faithful service he does not trust them completely: after every meal he locks up the dessert and the wine. He does not trust anybody; he shaves himself rather than employ a barber who might cut his throat.[25] And he occupies himself only with dead things, except for one small flower garden. Dust has accumulated everywhere, especially in the library, which he no longer uses.

Almost imperceptibly, Victor wins his uncle's affection. This is shown, on the part of the uncle, by greater trust and fewer restrictions. The climax of the story is the last dinner which uncle and nephew have together. From time to time lightning illuminates the uncle's face, symbolizing the deep emotion welling up in him (364). In the course of the conversation Victor remarks that one needs to love in order to be loved. In the uncle's outcry, "It is you I could have loved," regret for a wrongly lived life bursts forth with the strength of a dammed-up mountain stream. Although he feels deep pity for his uncle, Victor remains silent when questioned about returning this belated affection. The uncle feels that he has lived in vain, because he constitutes no link in the chain of generations; and with his death his individual being will be completely lost.[26]

The only thing the uncle feels he can still do is to prevent a similar fate for his nephew. He advises him to marry, and to do so very young. He also advises him, in the spirit of Goethe's *Wilhelm Meister,* not to start his career immediately, but first to broaden his experience. *"Jeder ist um sein selbst willen da"* (Every man exists, first of all, for himself [369]), but *"da sein"* (to exist) means activation of *all* of one's faculties; then, and only then, one will be of the best possible use to others. Compassion, sympathy, and willingness to help, the uncle argues, are included in the faculties which demand to be activated. This development of all our faculties, in the opinion of the uncle—and that of Stifter—can best be achieved by devoting oneself to agriculture.

Through the generosity of his uncle, Victor can, if he wishes, join Stifter's family of gentleman-farmers. After four years of travel he marries Hanna. The uncle does not accept Victor's personal invitation to his wedding. The story closes with the old man sitting alone on his island while the others celebrate, just as we saw him sitting there in the first chapter. He is compared to the fruitless fig tree of the biblical parable, withering and finally thrown away by the gardener, leaving no trace behind. Nothing earthly is immortal, but the childless man perishes sooner because he is already dying while still living and breathing. It is easy to recognize in these words the author's own anguish.

There is no doubt that Stifter accomplished his aim in *Der Hagestolz:* to create a great, somberly magnificent character.[27] The uncle adds refreshing variety to Stifter's usually gentle characters. He claims, in rather un-Stifterian fashion, that violence may, at times, be necessary in order to be really helpful and effective. The silent, majestic mountains are the right foil for this rugged, tragic character. But the painter Stifter may also have chosen the setting just to revel in the everchanging play of colors, light and shadow, the innumerable hues of hazy blue and gray, and the reflections in the lake. As a painter, Stifter had often struggled to render the grandeur and beauty of mountain landscapes, but he never succeeded as well as he did in writing *Der Hagestolz.*[28]

Der Waldsteig (The Woodland Path), together with *Die drei Schmiede ihres Schicksals,* is Stifter's only attempt at humor in fiction. Both were written in 1844. But although *Der Waldsteig* is moderately funny in parts, it is really a serious story based on three of Stifter's favorite themes: the great human value and strength of simple children of nature, the healing power of nature (its beauty, sunshine, and pure, fragrant air), the rightness of life lived in accordance with the laws of nature, which include marriage.

Tiburius, the main character, is a rich heir and hypochondriac. He has inherited this trait from his father. His education by an overanxious mother, an honest but foolish bachelor tutor and an equally foolish bachelor uncle did not help matters. Thus, Tiburius grew up to be a severe neurotic, a term unknown in Stifter's time, for which the word fool *(Narr)* still served. The clinical picture of the neurosis and its symptoms is to the point: hypochondria, withdrawal, fears and regrets, neglect of one's appearance, clinging to established habits and habitats. It is as if Stifter had anticipated some of his own later suffering.

In Tiburius's neighborhood there lives a physician who no longer practices, but leads what he considers the healthiest life, that of a gardener and farmer. In the beginning, after he had settled on his farm, people still came to see him as a doctor, but since he prescribed only "natural things"—hard work, better food, fresh air—instead of

pending

medicine, people called him a fool and lost confidence in him.[29] That epithet arouses Tiburius's curiosity. He seeks out the doctor, who, after several visits, advises him to go to a spa, find a girl, and marry. After elaborate preparations, Tiburius goes to a watering place in the mountains. On one of his daily walks there, taken only for the sake of the prescribed exercise, he gets lost in the woods. Luckily, he encounters a woodcutter, who takes him back to the village, slowing his pace and going out of his way, thus showing great consideration for the exhausted man. Recovered from his adventure, Tiburius returns every day to the spot where he went astray. He takes up drawing, one of the many hobbies he had started in his loneliness. One day he sees a beautiful peasant girl sitting on the stone where he often sat to draw. The girl, whose name is Maria, has been picking wild strawberries, still ripening in the mild autumn sun. They meet again, he falls in love with her, and the following year, when he returns to the spa, they marry. He is by now completely cured. He travels with his wife for three years, then settles in the mountains, which he has learned to love, and where the doctor joins him. He discards all hypochondriac notions, imbibes air and sunshine, and lives happily ever after.

The modern reader will believe Stifter when he says that Tiburius's physical and mental well-being improved with every day in the mountains, but it is hardly credible that such a deep-seated neurosis can be completely cured through fresh air, sunshine, exercise, and marriage to a child of nature.[30] It is difficult to tell whether in *Der Waldsteig* Stifter introduced the happy ending because he was following his literary models, Tieck and E. T. A. Hoffmann,[31] because he felt that the light, humorous tone called for it, or because he wanted to prove his point about the healing power of nature. Whatever the answer to this question, the modern reader will be more interested in the description of the neurosis than in its improbable cure. What he will enjoy most is the setting for the cure. Before his journey to the spa, Tiburius had never seen the mountains, their streams and woods. When he sees them for the first time, he is intoxicated, but also frightened. Gradually he grows familiar with them and is more and more enchanted with their stillness and grandeur. Since Tiburius gets lost and can find his way a second time only by paying attention to every detail, Stifter can indulge in minute description. Stifter's love of details also finds a natural outlet in Tiburius's pedantry. The ceremonious style which becomes more and more characteristic of Stifter's later work is very appropriate for Tiburius's speech. It is questionable whether it is equally appropriate for Maria, the child of nature. Stifter himself felt that the scene where Tiburius loses his way in the woods was probably the best part of the story, but had doubts whether he had fully succeeded in the scenes with Maria *(Br I, 271)*.

With human beings to be human, with the loftier spirits among them to love what is sublime; to enjoy God's creation, not to scorn what is of this earth; ever to devote oneself to useful pursuits; like Maria in *The Sisters*, not to disdain planting vegetables and fertilizing flower beds, yet to be noble, self-sacrificing; finally, to have an invisible fellowship, as it were, with sensitive, great minds—this was more or less the basis of my writings.

Thus wrote Stifter to Louise von Eichendorff on March 23, 1852. *Die Schwestern*, published in the *Iris* for 1846, was the original title of *Zwei Schwestern*, one of the lesser-known stories in the *Studien*. The reason for this neglect may be its great length, epic breadth, and loosely knit composition. The work is almost a novel and in many ways points toward the later *Nachsommer*. In not being familiar with *Zwei Schwestern*, one misses some of Stifter's most beautiful nature scenes and an important link between his earlier and later style. Besides, his basic philosophy of life—renunciation and useful activity—comes clearly to the fore in this *Novelle*.

The narrator, whose name, Otto Falkhaus, is revealed only toward the end of the story, meets an older man, Rikar, first in a stagecoach and later in a Vienna inn. Out of these chance encounters develops a lasting friendship, as happens in *Brigitta, Kalkstein, Der Nachsommer, Witiko, Die Nachkommenschaften*. On a rainy evening, they attend a concert of the famous prodigies, the Milanollo sisters. Both men are deeply moved; Rikar even weeps uncontrollably. On the way home he utters the mysterious words, "O unhappy father, unhappy father!" (477). Several years later, Falkhaus visits Rikar in his home above Lake Garda. His way leads him across a rocky plateau, and we experience with him, as we do in *Brigitta* and *Kalkstein*, the somber beauty peculiar to a vast expanse of land without houses, trees, shrubs, meadows, or fields:

In allen Stufen des matten Grün, Grau und Blau lag das fabelhafte Ding hinaus; schwermütig dämmernde, schwebende, webende Tafeln von Farben stellten sich hin, und die Felsen rissen mattschimmernde Lichtzuckungen hinein; und wo das Land bloss lag und etwa nur Sand und Gerölle hatte, drangen Flächen fahlen Glanzes oder sanft gebrochene Farbtöne vor. Draussen über allem duftete ruhig und schwach rötlich ein Berg. . . . Von ihm gingen zwei langgestreckte, feurige Wolkenbänke weg, die von der bereits zum Untergange neigenden Sonne angezündet waren und das schwache, trübe Grün des südlichen Himmels neben sich hatten, das so sanft glänzte und oben in ein flammendes Blau überlief. (513)

This passage is cited in German as a particularly good example of the impressionistic style of Stifter, the painter. Any translation can only be an approximation.[32]

Throughout the part of the story which takes place above Lake Garda, the modern reader is seized with desperate longing for the immense grandeur, solitude, and stillness of this landscape. Shortly before Falkhaus comes to Rikar's home, he sees the lonely figure of a girl in white sitting quietly in the shadow of a big, black, solitary rock crowned by a dead pine tree. In the faintly golden evening sky, high above the pine tree, an eagle hovers like a black insect. Later, we learn that the girl is Camilla, one of the two sisters, and the strong symbolism of the scene then becomes evident.

During his stay, Falkhaus makes friends with Rikar's small family, his wife Victoria and his two daughters Camilla and Maria. The sisters resemble each other very much, but whereas Maria is healthy, sun-tanned (too much so for the taste of the time!), active, and outgoing, Camilla is pale, slender, delicate, and withdrawn. There is a languishing look about her, especially in the first version of the story.[33] The father having lost his fortune through no fault of his own, Maria has saved the family from financial ruin by raising fruit, vegetables, and flowers. Like Brigitta, she has wrested everything from a seemingly infertile soil. She has been so successful that she was able to have their delapidated house repaired and to provide the family with the luxuries of the leisure class—an achievement which strikes one as improbable. She has been greatly assisted in her endeavors by their neighbor, Alfred Mussar, who has become their closest friend. Camilla does not share her sister's work; she has given her life to music, to the violin. She plays it so enchantingly that Falkhaus can compare her only to Theresa Milanollo. His idyllic sojourn in the midst of this ideal family is pleasantly interrupted by Mussar's return from a trip. For every member of the family he has selected with much thought valuable gifts which they most generously share with Falkhaus. The thoughtful, loving exchange of gifts is important in Stifter's work as part of his preference for symbolic gestures over more direct, effusive manifestations of feeling. Visits to Mussar's farm ensue. There we learn that he is a self-made man who has become rich through consistent effort and frugal living. This is a frequent pattern with Stifter, and once his heroes have succeeded, there are no limits to the size of their fortunes and to their spending, as there would be in reality. Thus, having inherited a run-down property, Mussar now possesses not only a model farm and a beautiful house with some exquisite Italian paintings, but also collections of samples of grain from all over the world, of watercolors of flowers growing in grainfields, and of agricultural tools, "a peaceful arsenal of the earth, so to speak" (609).[34]

When Mussar is alone with Falkhaus, he expounds his views on nature. There are in nature, he says, degrees of relationship to man, with minerals being the farthest removed from the human realm. Plants are closer, and animals living above ground—pale mirror images of ourselves—still more so, "but the closest to man is always man" (613). "The proper study for man is mankind," writes Ottilie in her diary after a similar discussion in Goethe's *Wahlverwandtschaften* (Part II, Chapter 7). Of course, Mussar goes on to say, nature as a whole (of which man is a part) occupies the highest place. She is the raiment of God, whom we can see only in her; she is the language through which alone He speaks to us; she is the expression of majesty and order. But she moves in accordance with her own great laws, which are far removed from us; she has no regard for us and does not condescend to share our weaknesses. We can only stand and admire. The little word "but" gives Stifter away. Here, as in the introduction to *Abdias* and the philosophical aside in *Die Mappe,* he wrestles with the incompatibility of God's love and benevolence and nature's absolute indifference toward us. The God who emerges from these reflections is a distant God who communicates with us through a language which we do not really understand, not the personal God whom we meet in Stifter's letters.

After Falkhaus's visit to Mussar, the story comes quickly to a head. Alfred asks for Maria's hand. Although she loves him, she rejects him, because Camilla loves him too. Maria knows that she is stronger than Camilla, whose natural sensitivity has been heightened through her music. With almost superhuman strength, Alfred and Maria control their feelings. Alfred stays for dinner. His last words at departing are, "When I come back, I shall bring the auricula seed and some of the new bulbs" (618). This sounds extremely trivial, but what Stifter means to say is that we can conquer our personal sorrow by devoting ourselves to our tasks, and that our individual grief is unimportant in comparison with nature's eternal cycle. Stifter had expressed the latter thought twice before, in *Die Mappe* and *Der Hagestolz*.[35]

In the first version of *Zwei Schwestern*, Mussar is less stoic: upon leaving, he tells Maria that he will not see her again, although through correspondence he wants to continue to help her. In contrast to the first version, the *Studien* version has a happy ending. When Falkhaus visits the Rikar family two years later, Camilla has married Alfred. She has become healthier, more domestic and active, and her music more joyous and vigorous. The dichotomy between life and art has been healed—too easily, it seems. Either Camilla is not the great artist whose innermost being is affected by her art, as she has been presented throughout the story, or the change is improbable, untrue. In the first version, Stifter stressed the destructive, almost sinister power of art, especially music, over a sensitive being. The problem of the artist remained unsolved, and we are left with the impression that Camilla may die prematurely because of her art, like Antonie in E. T. A. Hoffmann's *Rat Krespel*. Speaking of the happy ending of the *Studien* version, Lunding remarks that one should not blame Stifter for seeing something salutary in the restoration of Camilla's inner balance. But such a recovery seems to him of doubtful value for the true artist, and we should be grateful that Stifter himself never achieved this inner peace which he so ardently courted.[36]

As seems fitting, *Der beschriebene Tännling* (The Inscribed Fir Tree), the last of Stifter's *Studien*, leads us back to the scenes of his childhood, the immediate surroundings of Oberplan, with the bluish, hazy ribbon of the Bohemian woods at the horizon. The impatient reader may be deterred from finishing the story by the topographical details introduced at the beginning. Local folklore, secular and sacred legends play an important role. The people are devout Catholics, and the story centers on a miraculous statue of the Virgin Mary, a Pietà, in a little church. Although many miracles have happened in the past, none occurs in the story itself, quite in contrast to the works of some modern Catholic writers—Paul Claudel and Gertrud von Le Fort, for instance. Religion belongs to the people as part of their tradition and is thoroughly integrated into their lives and the natural rhythm of the seasons. The day of first confession for children is set before Easter Sunday, so that the children may be as pure as their clothes, the church banners, and spring. And people firmly believe that the Virgin Mary in the little church will fulfill every wish brought to her on the day of first confession. She fulfills wishes on other days too, but only if they are not in conflict with the moral order, not "confused or wrong" *(verwirrt oder verkehrt)*.

The protagonist of the story is the woodcutter Hanns, and Stifter has put into him his own lasting affection and respect for this profession. Hanns is in love with Hanna, the extraordinarily beautiful daughter of a poor widow. Hanna's fear of coming into contact with any dust or dirt is not a sign of utmost purity, as it is with Camilla in *Zwei Schwestern,* but rather of being a misfit in her class, a rural counterpart to the heroine of Maupassant's short story "The Necklace." On the day of her first confession, Hanna tells her playmates of a vision she has had while praying to the Holy Virgin. She saw the Virgin looking at her and pointing to the splendor of her raiment. Hanna, sharing popular belief, is now convinced that all this splendor will be hers in later life. Since she does not look at the sorrowful face of the Pietà, but only at her beautiful robe, it is easy to realize that her "vision" is nothing but a projection of her own wishes.

A great hunt and festival, held in these otherwise quiet regions, rudely interrupt Hanns' and Hanna's love. The description of that part of the hunt where animals are driven into nets, is one of the few places in Stifter's work where he takes human cruelty into account, the "tiger in man" of which he speaks in his tale *Zuversicht.* During the festivities, Hanna happens to stand next to Guido, a young nobleman, whose beauty matches hers. As if provoking fate, the people shout repeatedly: "That is the most beautiful couple of all." Hanna and Guido meet again, and soon rumor has it that they are going to be married. Hanns, who has had to be away working in the woods, hears of this only upon his return. He sees Hanna and Guido together and learns that at the battue with which the hunt closes, Guido will take his stand at the so-called *"beschrie-bene Tännling,"* a fir tree with lovers' inscriptions. Hanns sets out to find him there and kill him. We guess his intention, however, exclusively from his actions: the fetching and whetting of his ax, his going to the tree, his praying to the Pietà on his way. We are not told what he is praying for. His movements seem mechanical, as if he were propelled by one strong impulse. As Lunding has pointed out, this impression is achieved through constant repetition of the same verbs *(er ging, er nahm)* and the division of each of his actions into its obvious components. What to the superficial reader may seem artificial and boring is, in fact, a subtle artistic device.[37]

After reaching the tree, Hanns sits down and falls asleep. He too has a vision, in which the tree seems to have grown and reaches into heaven. High up in the branches stands the Pietà, looking down at him. Her glance is inexorably stern. At that moment, Hanns wakes up. Meantime the moon has risen and stands almost directly above the tree. The branches glisten, and between them long beams of light, like silver ribbons, reach down to Hanns. (The Pietà in the church has silver ribbons hanging from the bouquet in her hand.) The light is dim—the word actually used is "dubious" *(zweifelhaft)*—just enough to discern objects. Although the moment of awakening is distinct, dream blends with reality. As with Hanna, Hanns' vision can be interpreted psychologically: the stern look of the Virgin is a projection of his own conscience. "What I asked for, must have been wrong" *(etwas Verworrenes),* he says as soon as he is fully awake (688). Others among Stifter's heroes—Jodok in *Die Narrenburg,* the colonel in *Die Mappe,* the uncle in *Der Hagestolz*—also think of murder in the first onslaught of emotion, but none goes through with it. Hanns, a broken man, returns to his place of work in order to hide during the rest of the festivities. Guido and Hanna marry.

Many years later, Hanna passes through the region and meets Hanns without recognizing him. Her pallor and quietness seem to indicate that she has missed real happiness. He has with him his sister's three orphaned children, whom he has adopted. Hanna throws a silver dollar to the poor man. In the first version of the story, Hanns, who does recognize her, picks up the coin and throws it under the wheels of the departing carriage. In the *Studien* version, in line with the general softening of the second versions, he has it set in a frame as a votive offering to the Virgin.

The story closes with a discussion of the Virgin's powers. Hanna's former playmates remark that the mercy of the Holy Virgin had clearly demonstrated itself in her. A very old man refutes them, saying that it was rather the Virgin's curse than her mercy which had shown itself in Hanna and that it was somebody else [Hanns] in whom the Virgin had shown her wisdom, mercy, and miraculous power. The word "curse" is startling in connection with the Holy Virgin. Stifter may have wished to imply that some old pagan concepts were still surviving among the peasants; or, more probably, he may simply have wished to leave no doubt about Hanna's not being happy in spite of the fulfillment of all her material wishes. Much as we admire Stifter's art of omission or his subtle hints, here, for once, we would like a more overt statement of the causes of Hanna's assumed unhappiness. Had she grown spiritually, so that material things had become unimportant to her? Did her conscience trouble her? Was she childless? Had the gentle Guido changed? How much is Hanna to blame for her fate? How much is owing to circumstances? It is this lack of "incisiveness in the presentation of the theme," which Blackall gives as one of the reasons for not counting the story among Stifter's best works.[38]

Der Waldgänger (The Wanderer in the Forest), which Stifter wrote while he was revising the third and fourth volume of the *Studien,* but did not include in them, has been called a story of remorse.[39] It could just as well be called a story of loneliness. The setting of the first part is the melancholy landscape of Stifter's native woods with their isolated small gray houses. All the people in the story are lonely people, whom fate, at the very best, grants a brief respite from their isolation. The words *allein, einsam, vereinsamt, vereinzelt* (alone, lonely, isolated) are key words in the story. The introduction is rather long, comprising about a third of the first chapter, "Am Waldwasser." Stifter muses on his long-lost love and youth and then goes on to the exact description of the country (where we shall meet the *Waldgänger*), the landscape, the people, their customs and legends. The *Waldgänger,* Georg, is a solitary old man who roams through the woods (whence his name) collecting butterflies and different types of moss. He wins the love and companionship of a small boy, only to lose it again, in spite of the boy's innocent words: "Father, I shall never leave you as long as I live" (III, 428). The boy has to go away to learn a trade, and the old man, overwhelmed by grief, leaves the region, never to be seen again.

The second chapter, "Am Waldhange," takes us far back into the past, into the lives of Georg and his wife Corona. Georg grows up as the only child of an elderly couple in a remote parsonage in northern Germany. He, too, has to leave his home for further education, and the parents, after a brief visit from their son, are once more alone: "The parsonage made lively through his visit was as lonely as before. The loneliness was the same every day: it was the same lonely sun which shone every day on the roof of the house and, in the evening, always gilded the same spot on the church steeple" (440). The parents die while their son is away. Up to his thirtieth year Georg spends his life in absolute loneliness. He studies science and architecture and becomes a much-sought-after builder. As such he meets Corona, companion to a crotchety, heartless old countess, who wants part of her property remodeled. There is a good deal of implicit social criticism in the behavior of the countess. Corona's loneliness is, if possible, even greater than Georg's. Bitter experiences after her mother's death, when Corona was only sixteen, have driven her into utmost silence and isolation, but have also developed in her unusual strength of character, something unbending and uncompromising. It is this *"verödete Grösse"* (desolate greatness) which attracts Georg. They marry. After frugal beginnings they build a beautiful house in beautiful surroundings—Stifter's constantly recurring dream. But their happiness is marred by their not having any children. This grief comes to a climax at a party (a rare event for them) where the still-beautiful Corona sits *"vereinsamt und vereinzelt"* among proud, happy parents. Several weeks later—it is the thirteenth year of their marriage—Corona comes to her husband with the strange suggestion of divorce, so that each can remarry and have children. Georg intuitively knows that Corona is wrong, but after some time accepts her proposal.

In the third chapter, "Am Waldrande," we learn that Georg has remarried, though without love. For Stifter, to marry without real affection means sinning against "the true laws of nature" (IV, 791). Georg's wife has borne him two sons; he is now looking for a site to build a house in which to spend his old age. He is attracted by a place very similar to the one where he had so happily lived with Corona. There, exactly thirteen years after they had separated, he meets Corona who, for the same reason, had been drawn to this locality. Their brief encounter is one of the most moving scenes

Stifter has written, masterly in its artistic economy. The couple exchange few words, but every gesture, every word, and every pause is meaningful. When Georg learns that Corona had not been able to go against her deepest feelings and remarry, speech fails him. After a short while, he stretches his hand out to her and says nothing but "Good night, Elizabeth." This is Corona's second name, which he had used during their marriage when he felt especially close to her.[40] For a precarious moment, the time of their separation is erased.

Back in his room at the inn, the fifty-year-old man weeps the whole night. He realizes for the first time how wrong he had been in yielding to Corona, what a "great sin" he had committed. He never settles down anywhere; his wife dies, and his two sons leave. One son almost never writes; the other only every two or three years. It is the law of nature, Stifter says, that children leave their parents, as young branches strive away from the old withered branch without ever looking back (429, 492). There is no Indian summer for Georg and Corona. He is too ashamed to look for her; besides, he does not know whether she, too, has left the place of their encounter. He becomes the eternal wanderer whom we have met at the beginning. He has reduced his earthly possessions to a minimum, for material things are poor substitutes for human warmth and happiness. There is probably no sadder ending in Stifter's work than the picture of the two old people, each once more utterly alone. We do not even know when and where and how they die. The thought that one may have to pay so dearly for a mistake made in good faith is almost unbearable. This tragic story is a far cry from Stifter's later—often determined—optimism and ought to be better known than it is at present.[41]

CHAPTER 4

Bunte Steine

*B*UNTE STEINE (Colored Stones), the collection of stories which followed the *Studien,* was published in 1853 with the subtitle *Ein Festgeschenk* (A Holiday Gift). Its creation spans a decade: the oldest of the stories, *Bergmilch,* appeared in a Vienna journal in 1843, entitled *Wirkungen eines weissen Mantels* (Effects of a White Cloak). *Katzensilber* (Mica) was probably written as late as 1852. Stifter's plan to write stories for children also goes back a decade, but it was only after the work on the *Studien* approached its close early in 1849 that he seriously took up this idea. With the exception of *Katzensilber,* however, he did not create new stories for the book; they were merely new versions of stories already published.

Stifter points out in his Introduction that the stories are suitable not for children, but for young people.[1] It has often been remarked that they are actually not *for* children but *about* children; yet even this is only partially true, for the protagonists in *Kalkstein,* in the first part of *Turmalin,* and in *Bergmilch* are neither children nor young people. In fact, the well-intentioned custom of reading *Bergkristall* with German students in the seventh or eighth grade does a great disservice to Stifter. Children of this age want action in their reading; the magnificent nature descriptions bore them, as a recent survey by the author of this book has clearly shown. Neither can we take at face value Stifter's explanation of the title: that these stories are a collection of trifles to be enjoyed by young people, as he had enjoyed his childhood collection of beautiful, but not valuable, stones. The themes of the stories, especially those of *Kalkstein, Turmalin,* and *Bergmilch,* are too serious to be called trifles, nor does their artistic merit warrant such a modest evaluation. With a less serious and honest writer than Stifter, one might call this attitude flirting with the public.

Bunte Steine is usually at the center of any discussion of Stifter's work, not so much in regard to any of its stories as because of its Preface. Altogether, this is probably the best-known piece of

Stifter's writing, partly because it is short enough to be wholly or partially included in any anthology, but even more so because, in it, Stifter summarizes his philosophical and esthetic views. The opening sentence, "I have on one occasion been accused of describing only minutiae and of always choosing ordinary people for my characters," makes it quite obvious that the Preface is a reply to Hebbel's attack on Stifter.

As early as 1847, Stifter had been asked by the editor of the *Augsburger Allgemeine Zeitung* to give his views on Hebbel. In his answer, Stifter said that he could not do so publicly because he did not like to hurt anybody's feelings unnecessarily, and so restricted his criticism to this private communication. He did not deny Hebbel's talent and recognized in his work "bold images, keen ideas, even tragic flashes." All this, nevertheless, seemed futile to him, since Hebbel lacked the only thing which matters: moral depth and dignity. What Stifter objected to most was Hebbel's dwelling upon the "monstrous, the bizarre, the immoderate." The ostentatious show of strength in Hebbel's characters seemed to Stifter nothing but weakness in disguise, whereas the mark of strength is "moderation, self-control, ethical orientation." He cites Holofernes in *Judith,* whom he calls the biggest clown on the stage known to him. Stifter's compatriot Nestroy very wittily ridiculed this swashbuckling megalomaniac in his travesty, *Judith und Holofernes.* Hebbel, Stifter continues in his letter, has a tragic bent, but because of his lack of moral depth, seizes upon the repugnant instead of the tragic. His plays leave the morally unsophisticated reader distressed because he has fallen upon such "unreal" people; there remains something desperately unsolved at the end. (*Br I,* 247–50.)

Further discussion of Stifter's views on Hebbel would be inappropriate in this context. This writer, however, confesses to having sensations similar to Stifter's on reading Hebbel's plays, except for *Agnes Bernauer.* It would be interesting to know how many Stifter admirers are able also to appreciate Hebbel. Among modern German writers, Oskar Loerke, for one, agrees with Stifter's judgment: he concedes that there are some great feelings and thoughts in Hebbel's plays, but still calls them "monstrous" as a whole.[2]

It is probably an oversimplification to explain this controversy by the contrast between northener and southerner. According to

Stifter, however, Grillparzer and many other Viennese shared his views. Nestroy's parody also seems to lend support to such an explanation. But aside from the contrast between north and south, Stifter and Hebbel, as individuals, were diametrically opposed natures and could not be fair to each other. Hebbel, being much more aggressive, however, had no scruples about attacking Stifter in public, as, for example, in the uncharitable epigram, "Die alten Naturdichter und die neuen":

> Do you know why you are so successful in depicting beetles
>   and buttercups?
> Because you do not know man, because you do not see the stars!
> If you looked deep into hearts, how could you rave about beetles?
>   If you saw the solar system, say, what would a bouquet be to you?
> But that's the way it had to be; so that you could deal in small things
>   So well, nature wisely kept the big things from you.[3]

It is the nature of clichés to be repeated endlessly. This one certainly was and has greatly affected the appreciation of Stifter. For a long time, people were kept from reading him at all—some still are—or read him with preconceived notions. Actually, Stifter very seldom describes flowers and insects minutely. It is true that he loves to dwell on forest scenes, but they relate to the stories and the human heart, as in *Der Hochwald, Der Waldsteig, Der Waldgänger, Der beschriebene Tännling.* In most stories and novels where Stifter describes nature in detail, it is in connection with human endeavor: that of the collector, the scientist, or, especially, the tiller of the soil, since, as we have seen, the ordering of nature, making her fruitful, is for him the noblest and most gratifying human occupation. Even the most perfunctory reader of Stifter soon discovers how superficial and unjust Hebbel's criticism is: sunrises and sunsets, moonlit and starry nights far outnumber "beetles and buttercups." The more careful and unprejudiced reader will notice that, as a rule, in his nature descriptions Stifter is not a miniature painter, but an impressionist, working almost exclusively with bold brush strokes, light and shadow, color contrasts. He will detect Stifter's love of sweeping vistas seen from a high vantage point, and of atmospheric phenomena, such as cloud formations and thunderstorms. In the discussion of *Zwei Schwestern,* we have already cited an example of his impressionistic style.[4] The weakness in his nature descriptions is of a different kind: it is difficult to follow without a map his occasionally long and rather tiresome topographical details.

It certainly would be wrong to interpret the Preface chiefly as a reply to Hebbel's attack. It is rather Stifter's philosophical, moral, and esthetic manifesto. His concept of what he considered truly great had developed before Hebbel's attack, and he had expressed it twice (in 1846 and 1847) in almost the same words.[5] For him all gentle, slowly changing, ever recurring phenomena are great phenomena, which seem insignificant, but which in their eternal repetition form the foundation of the universe: the breezes of the air, flowing water, ripening grain, the waves of the ocean, the first green of spring, the light of the sky and the stars. More spectacular phenomena, such as lightning, hurricanes, volcanos, and earthquakes, are lower on his scale of values, because they are isolated and occasional. Primitive, ignorant man is overawed by them, whereas the enlightened scientist is chiefly interested in the general laws of the universe because they represent *"das welterhaltende Gesetz"* (the principle which maintains the universe). Then Stifter makes an analogy to human life, and we are at the very core of his feeling and thinking. Here too, it is the unending, daily repetition of seemingly insignificant attitudes and actions which counts, and not the so-called great deeds, because they may be the result of violent emotions and as destructive as the corresponding phenomena in nature. Thus, he writes:

A whole life long of justice, simplicity, self-mastery, rational conduct, useful activity in the place to which one is called, admiration of the beautiful, together with a calm, serene death—this life I consider great. Strong agitations of the soul, raging anger, desire for revenge, a mind on fire that demands action in tearing down, changing, destroying, and in this excitement often throws its life away—all these I do not consider greater but actually of less significance, since they are only the results of single and unilateral forces, as are storms, volcanos, earthquakes. We strive to perceive the gentle law *(das sanfte Gesetz)* whereby mankind is guided. (III, 10)

Stifter distinguishes between those forces which aim at the development of the individual and those which aim at the preservation of mankind. The latter have a restraining influence on the former; and in case of conflict, they have the right of way, as it were. It is the law of these forces, the law of justice and of morality *(Sitte)* which requires that it be possible for every individual to coexist with other men, respected and unharmed, to pursue his lofty human course, to win the love and admiration of his fellow human beings, and to be treasured like a jewel, as every man is a jewel for all other men. However powerful this universal law is in great historical movements and heroic actions, it is most firmly rooted in ordinary human actions. The moral law preserves mankind in the same way as the laws of nature uphold the universe: the *"menschenerhaltende Gesetz"* and the *"welterhaltende Gesetz"* run parallel. We feel elevated and confirmed in our humanity whenever history moves toward a greater realization of this universal law of justice and morality, but we are repelled by movements which strive toward one-sided and selfish goals. We consider them small and unworthy of man, powerful and terrible though they may be. It is not difficult to recognize in these words Stifter's deep disappointment in the Revolution of 1848.

In the Preface to *Bunte Steine,* the scientist, the humanist, the artist, and the religious man in Stifter meet: the scientist who wants to find the universal laws of nature; the humanist who wants to find the universal laws for mankind, the balance between the right of the individual and the good of all; and the religious man for whom the terms small or big are nonexistent as they are for God. "God does not know the words small or big," Stifter writes in 1853; "for Him there is only that which is right" (*Br II,* 190). The German mystic, Angelus Silesius, has expressed the same theocentric, as opposed to an anthropocentric, view. Nothing could be more akin to Stifter than Silesius's verse: "In Gott ist alles Gott: ein einzigs Würmelein,/Das ist in Gott so viel als tausend Gotte sein." (In God everything is God, a single tiny worm/Is as important to God as a thousand Gods.)

An anthropocentric view of the universe, which Stifter repeatedly attacked—in *Der Hochwald, Der Nachsommer, Witiko,* the last version of *Die Mappe*—clouds our vision as much as do our individual passions: both prevent us from entering into the essence of things. In his Introduction to *Bunte Steine,* Gustav Wilhelm has shown many parallels between Stifter's views on the small and the great and those of Herder, Goethe, Jean Paul, and Wilhelm von Humboldt. Although Stifter knew the works quoted by Wilhelm, there is probably as much a priori affinity as there is direct influence. The emphasis Stifter placed on his concept of the truly great, his revaluation of conventional values is revealed in the numerous repetitions and variations of this theme.[6]

More important than all of Stifter's theoretical statements is the fact that his most moving figures, originating in his innermost being, are convincing incarnations of the "gentle law." The emphasis on the seemingly insignificant, but actually great character, on the ordinary round of everyday life, also makes Stifter a representative of "Poetic" or "Middle-Class Realism" *(Bürgerlicher Realismus)*, as the literary style of his time has been called. We are reminded of Stifter when we read in Jeremias Gotthelf's *Uli der Pächter* that the number of people who experience only the "so-called small things" is infinitely larger than the number of Herculeses, Alexanders and Napoleons, and that these things are most important for the wise man.[7] Stifter could well have written Flaubert's sentence: "One can put immense love in the story of a blade of grass."[8]

Granit, the first story of *Bunte Steine,* takes place on Stifter's native soil, as does the last of the *Studien.* A tale of his boyhood, it opens and closes with the old stone in front of Stifter's birthplace on which he and his grandfather liked to sit. One day, when the boy Stifter is sitting on the stone, the cart-grease peddler Andreas puts some of his lubricant on the little boy's bare feet, as a kind of practical joke, meant to do no harm. But when his feet leave ugly spots on the freshly scrubbed floor, the boy is punished by his mother, who is usually very kind. In order to comfort the boy, the grandfather takes him along on an errand to a neighboring village. On the way to and from the village, he tells him a story which happened at the time of the last plague in southern Bohemia. He finishes it upon their return, resting on the old stone. While they walk, he points out the places where the events occurred, skillfully linking the present to the past. During the plague, says the grandfather, a family of pitch-makers went high up into the woods in order to escape it. Only one brother of the family did not stay with them. This was Andreas, the ancestor of the cart-grease peddler by that name. Flight from the plague did not help the pitch-maker and his family: they all died of it, except one small son, Joseph, who managed to survive with the resources at his disposal, meager as they were. One day, while wandering in the woods, he came upon a little girl lying unconscious in the midst of some blackberry bushes. She was ill of the plague, the only survivor of her family, who had also fled to the woods. He tenderly nursed her back to health and led her out of the big forest. The boy was finally reunited with his uncle

Andreas. Relatives of the little girl (Magdalena was her name) learned of her whereabouts and fetched her. Many years laters, as a beautiful young maiden, she returned to her rescuer, dressed in a white dress and black coat, as she had been when he had first found her. She took the youth with her to her castle and married him later.

This happy ending is already found in the otherwise fundamentally different first version of the story, called *Die Pechbrenner.* The plan of the pitch-maker to ward off any intruder who might bring the plague to his refuge, which is reduced to a mere intention in the second version, is stark reality in the first. When Magdalena's family, gone astray in the woods, approaches the pitch-maker for help, he throws a bundle of food at their feet but tells them not to come any closer if they value their lives. A burning beam in his hand clearly shows that he would carry out his threat. But Joseph has pity on them and shelters them in a nearby hut against the express orders of his father not to go close to the strangers. When the pitch-maker's family is stricken by the plague and the father finds out about the hut, he punishes his son in the most cruel fashion. He exposes him on a steep rock with enough food and water for two days. The father's immolation of the only son left to him and the laconic orders he gives him on the way to the rock remind one strongly of Mérimée's famous story, "Mateo Falcone." After two days, the mother asks for mercy, but it is too late; both father and mother are stricken and die before the boy can be rescued. The child suffers agonies of fear on his lonely rock, and his repeated, anguished cries for his father on the evening of the second day show nothing of Stifter's usual restraint. If Magdalena, here also the only survivor of her family, had not found him on the third day, he would have perished. With great ingenuity on Joseph's part and quick learning on Magdalena's, they manage to exist for a few days. This ingenuity is much more plausible here, where Joseph is thirteen, than in the second version, where he is still a very small boy. Finally, Knut, a feeble-minded servant of the pitch-maker, recovers from the plague and helps the boy to get down.

In the first version, as Max Stefl has pointed out, we have a virtually "unknown" Stifter, who does not shrink from depicting the animal instinct of self-preservation in man. As he says in the much-quoted passage from *Zuversicht,* we are not aware of our tigerlike disposition, which exists next to the heavenly one, until the brutal power of facts awakens it (III, 808). In the first version, Stifter does not shrink from including such gruesome details as the terrible stench of the corpses, which prevents Joseph from getting provisions in their former dwelling, or the uncle's horror when, upon his return, he sees his brother's half-burned bones projecting from the charred hay. (Knut had set fire to the huts before leaving.) In the first version, Stifter does not have the grandfather speak of the plague as a divine punishment, as he does in the second. Yet, even in the second version he does not dwell on this point and use it as a text for a sermon, the way Gotthelf uses the flood in *Die Wassernot im Emmental*. Stefl suggests that the changes were made because Stifter wanted to tell the story in conformity with the character and philosophy of the grandfather, as he wrote to Heckenast on January 23, 1852.[9] But it is very likely that the Stifter of 1852 could no longer tolerate the harshness, the brutality, and the naturalism acceptable to the Stifter of 1848. In the same letter to Heckenast, he wrote that he wanted a spirit of purity and inwardness *(Innigkeit)* to prevail in the story. Whatever the reasons for the changes, the first version seems preferable in many respects: it is stronger and more dramatic, and there is a better balance between the space given to the present (the framework) and the past (the actual story).

In the opinion of this writer, *Kalkstein* (Limestone), the next story of *Bunte Steine,* deserves to be better known with the general reading public. Thomas Mann calls it *"unbeschreiblich eigenartig und von stiller Gewagtheit"* (completely unparalleled and quietly daring).[10] It is the best illustration of what Stifter had set up as "great" in his Preface: "A whole life of justice, simplicity, self-mastery, rational conduct, useful activity in the place to which one is called, admiration of the beautiful, together with a calm, serene death." In *Kalkstein,* he achieved the childlike quality, the simplicity of moral greatness and kindness which he admired so much in Grillparzer's *Novelle Der arme Spielmann.* There is no doubt that Grillparzer's story of the poor fiddler inspired Stifter to write his story of the poor priest—or poor benefactor, as he is called in the title of the first version; the resemblance is striking. In his book, *Der bürgerliche Realismus im 19. Jahrhundert,* Martini points out that, within this period, there exists a whole cycle of stories very

similar in character to the two mentioned above. One could probably call them illustrations of the beatitude: "Blessed are the meek:
for they shall inherit the earth," and one might add to the German
works Flaubert's *Un Coeur simple.*

Kalkstein is the story of a poor priest who dedicates his whole
life to his calling and to the task of saving money for a noble purpose. He wants a new schoolhouse built so that the children will
not have to cross a little river which regularly inundates the surrounding country. Since he does not tell anybody of his goal, his
frugal living earns him the reputation of a miser. It is only after his
death that his moral greatness is revealed. He is ignorant of the
world and is robbed three times of his savings before he puts them
in a bank. He does not realize either that the small sum he can save
even with the utmost thrift will never suffice for his purpose. But
rich people, touched by the unselfishness of this man after his will
has been opened, underwrite a sum large enough to fulfill his dream.
Evil is always futile, Stifter tells us: it is only the good which will
have a lasting effect, even if it is begun with insufficient means
(III, 131).

What is so admirable in this story is the fact that the figure of
the priest, in spite of its ideal quality, remains convincingly real
throughout. Stifter was well aware of the difficulty of making such
a moral character ring true (VI, 253–54). He is very careful to avoid
sermonizing. The Christ-like qualities of the priest, his humility,
gentleness, and love of children, are implicit in his way of life. The
priest is very sparing with his words, which are therefore all the
more effective. We become familiar with this lonely, seemingly
strange man through the observations of the narrator, a young
surveyor, who, in the course of the story, changes from a casual
acquaintance to a friend. This change is brought about mainly
through a thunderstorm, the hospitality necessitated by it, and an
extended illness of the priest. During his illness, though he is usually reserved, he tells his new friend his life story and also initiates
him into his project, mainly in order to entrust to him a third copy
of his will. This exaggerated precaution is all the more touching,
since, as we have already mentioned, the savings alone would not
have done much good. The incident of the approaching storm and
the resulting friendship of the main characters is repeated with a
slight nuance in *Der Nachsommer.*

The description of the priest is, as always with Stifter's figures, reduced to a few simple, impressive traits: his tall haggard form, clothed in black, his smooth brown, graying hair, and, as a kind of leitmotif, his serene blue eyes (III, 62, 64, 92, 122, 125). His immaculate, elegant shirt strangely contrasts with his worn-out clothes. His beautiful linen and a valuable, hand-carved crucifix are the only remainders of a better past. The linen is also a souvenir of a long-lost love. He is ashamed of this luxury, his only human weakness, and keeps pushing his wrist-ruffles back underneath his coat sleeves. His furnishings are of the utmost simplicity: he sleeps on a wooden bench with a Bible as his pillow. The food which he shares with his guest consists of milk, wild strawberries, and dark bread. But all is offered with kindness and not without dignity. In spite of his position as a clergyman, he is humble enough to brush his guest's clothes himself, since his servant has not yet come when his guest is ready to leave. His character is matched by the region in which he serves. The barren limestone hills form one of those unpretentious landscapes of which Stifter was so fond. They reveal their hidden, melancholy beauty only slowly to the careful observer, in the same way as the moral beauty of the priest only slowly reveals itself to his friend. He could probably have gotten a transfer to a better parish, but has come to love this landscape as does the narrator in the end. In his great humility, the priest also believes that other, more brilliant men deserve the better positions more than he.

A close comparison of *Kalkstein* with Grillparzer's *Der arme Spielmann* will bring out very clearly the specific character of Stifter's writing. At first glance, one sees only the similarities: two extremely self-effacing human beings who, in the eyes of the world, do not amount to much. Both are slow learners outdone by more gifted brothers. Both grow up motherless. In their youth both experience a tender but frustrated love, the memory of which will stay with them the rest of their lonely lives. Both come from well-to-do families but lose their fortune. However, they keep their self-respect and dignity. Neither minds his own safety and health when it is a question of saving small children during an inundation. But Stifter mitigates every single feature of Grillparzer's story. Whereas the poor fiddler is a complete failure, a beggar musician and pauper, the priest occupies a respected, although modest, position. In contrast to the poor fiddler, he is allowed to make up for the slow start in his education. The father and the brothers in Grill-parzer's story are harsh and unkind to the point of cruelty, whereas with Stifter, both father and brother are most kind and generous. The poor fiddler loses his fortune through the wiles of a scoundrel, the priest more through circumstances than human malice. In Grillparzer's story, the girl is the daughter of a grocer, a rather crude man, while with Stifter, she is the daughter of an impover-ished lady who runs a laundry for fine linen and lingerie of wealthy people.[11] With Grillparzer, the man and the girl are separated through differences in character—he is too meek for her; with Stifter, the young people are separated because of the mother's excessive concern with propriety, a foretaste of Victorian attitudes. In both stories the lovers think more of the security and happiness of the girls than of their own (*Urf.*, 258)[12] and accept their fate with-out bitterness. Throughout Grillparzer's story, the fiddler has more reason than the priest to become bitter and rebel against his fate, but he never does. He dies a victim of his own generosity, helping beyond his strength during the flood, whereas the priest dies after a long, patiently borne illness. One could easily list further differ-ences between Stifter's and Grillparzer's narratives, but, as we have tried to point out at the very beginning of our discussion, it is the same spirit of true moral greatness which animates both stories.

Together with *Die Narrenburg* and *Das alte Siegel, Turmalin* is one of three stories which treat the subject of infidelity. But whereas in *Die Narrenburg* the wife describes her moment of for-getfulness, and whereas in *Das alte Siegel* the growing love between Hugo and Cöleste is convincingly depicted, in *Turmalin* one lacon-ic sentence deals with the whole relationship: "Finally, Dall started an affair with the wife of the *Rentherr* and continued it for a while" (III, 141). Dall is a famous actor, and the *Rentherr,* his closest friend, is a man who lives on his private income. He is an eccentric who covers every inch of the walls of his room with portraits of celebrities and uses ladders and couches of different heights (both on rollers) to see them all equally well. He is a true dilettante, dab-bling in numerous hobbies. His wife does not share in these, but lives a very secluded, rather monotonous life in her rooms with their small child. Dall, however, takes a lively interest in his friend's hobbies and even has a special armchair made for himself in order to be comfortable on his frequent visits.

When the wife, in her anguish, tells her husband of the affair, he follows a behavior pattern which is already familiar to us from *Die Narrenburg, Die Mappe,* and *Der Hagestolz.*[13] In his first rage he wants to murder Dall, but when he cannot find him, he calms down, is willing to forgive his wife, and blames himself for having introduced the irresistible Dall into their home. But the wife cannot forgive herself and leaves both husband and baby. Nobody knows her whereabouts, not even Dall, whom the husband begs three times on his knees to tell him and to give her back to him. When the wife does not return, the *Rentherr* dismisses the servant, takes the little girl in his arms, and leaves too. Nobody knows where he goes, and after two years the authorities are obliged to open the apartment. In the beginning of the story, in typical Stifter fashion, the cleanliness of the wife's rooms is stressed; now, everything in the whole apartment is covered with dust. Moths flutter out of a closet, as they do in Flaubert's *Un Coeur simple* when the old maid opens the dead girl's wardrobe. In the wife's room, the plants have withered, the grandfather clock has stopped; in the husband's room, Dall's armchair stands in the middle, a relic of their former close relationship. We hear nothing about Dall's further life or what happened to the wife. In the second part of the story, there are some strong hints, however, that she has committed suicide.

The second part of the story, which takes place many years later, is given as a report by a woman friend of the narrator.[14] One day, this woman sees a strangely clad man in the street, accompanied by a girl with an enormous head, in equally strange clothes. We learn that the two live in the basement of a beautiful old house, now run-down. But it is only after the old man suddenly dies of an accident in his home that we are told that he is the former *Rentherr,* and the girl his daughter. We also learn that he had earned his bread as a wandering musician, a flutist; in this, as well as in the uncommon way he had played the flute, there are reminiscences of Grillparzer's *Der arme Spielmann.* Among the old man's papers are found some compositions which the girl had written at her father's request. The father had given her only two gloomy topics: to describe either himself lying dead on his bier or her mother, miserable, wandering about the world and finally committing suicide.

The woman takes the girl into her home and tries to counterbalance this weird education.

The critics do not agree on the value of the story, but according to Stefl, the majority find it relatively successful, a judgment to which we would like to subscribe. The chief weakness of the story lies in the rather sketchy way in which the relationships and feelings of the main characters are analyzed. Although we fully appreciate the symbolic value of inanimate objects in this story, the space given to their description seems somewhat out of balance with that given to psychological details. "Much is left unsaid: this 'dark' tale has the obscurity of reality, the same gaps of information," remarks David Luke, a recent translator of the story.[15] But should not art elucidate this obscurity? For instance, we should like to know why the husband, who loved his wife so much, did not share more of his life with her. We should also like to know what enabled the woman to leave her small child, what became of her, and whether Dall felt any remorse for having betrayed his best friend and destroyed his life. Another puzzling aspect of the story is the fact that the only completely innocent person, the girl, is hurt most. Of course we do not want to intimate that in real life this does not happen constantly; such an outcome seems, however, inconsistent with Stifter's Weltanschauung. The moral of the story, as given in the introductory passage, can only refer to the father, and not to the child:

> It [Turmalin] is like a sad letter that tells us to what extremity man may come when he dims the light of his reason, when he no longer understands life, when he abandons that inner law which is his steadfast guide along the right path, when he surrenders utterly to the intensity of his joys and sorrows, loses his foothold, and is lost in regions of experience which for the rest of us are almost wholly shrouded in mystery. (III, 133)[16]

Most typical of Stifter are the following features in Turmalin: the complete omission of any passionate scenes; the husband's conciliatory behavior; the matter-of-factness with which the narrator of the second part of the story and her husband fulfill their human duty toward the dead man and the orphaned girl; the de-emphasis of the tragic aspects of the story. The old man, whose constantly shifting eyes had betrayed his insanity, appears tranquil on his bier after his eyes are closed. The girl, through good care and an iodine cure, improves so much that her head even gets a

little smaller! Finally, she is able to earn most of her livelihood by
means of needlework, a feature which was added to the second
version. Less important perhaps, but still very characteristic of
Stifter, is the fascination which the slow disintegration of the old
house and the reassertion of nature's sway have for the minor character, Professor Andorf. This fascination leads us back to the early
Studien, Der Hochwald and *Die Narrenburg,* and the description
of the old monastery in *Der Hagestolz.*

The most interesting part of the story is probably that where the
narrator, with infinite patience and great insight into the psyche
of the shy girl, wins her confidence and leads her back to society.
After enlarging the scope of this part in the second version, Stifter
may have felt justified, as Gustav Wilhelm suggests, in including
the story in *Bunte Steine,* but it is still not a story for young people.[17]

If the critics do not agree on the literary merits of *Turmalin,* they
are unanimous in their high praise of *Bergkristall* (Rock Crystal),
the next story contained in *Bunte Steine.* Its great popularity is
revealed in the large number of translations and separate editions.[18]
The origin of the story affords us a rare insight into the workings of
poetic imagination. The idea for the story came to Stifter on a visit
with the geographer Simony in Hallstatt, in the Dachstein region
of the Alps. On a walk they met two small children selling wild
strawberries. Stifter bought the berries, but let the children eat
them and tell him about their day. They had taken food to their
grandfather on a mountain pasture, gathered the berries on their
way back and, surprised by a thunderstorm, had taken shelter
under a projecting rock. On the same walk, Simony told Stifter
about his winter visit to a nearby glacier, and the next day showed
him a rather exact picture of a glacial cave into which he had pene-
trated. Stifter looked at it for a long while and then suddenly said,
"In my imagination, I have now transplanted the children of yester-
day into this blue ice dome; what a contrast there would be between
their lovely, budding, freshly pulsing human life and the splendid
but gruesome, rigid, deadly cold setting!"[19]

The whole story is built on contrasts. There is first the contrast
between the little mountain village of Gschaid and the much bigger
and wealthier village of Millsdorf in the valley on the other side of
a moderately high mountain ridge. The children's father is a shoe-
maker from Gschaid, their mother the daughter of a rich dyer from

Millsdorf. The people of Gschaid have never fully accepted her. There is also the contrast between the two children: the boy Konrad, a few years older than his sister Sanna, is very serious and intelligent for his age. Sanna's essential characteristic is infinite confidence in the knowledge, insight, and strength of her brother. Since the boy is so reliable, he is allowed in good weather to take his little sister to the grandparents in Millsdorf, three hours away.

Thus, on the day before Christmas (the title of the first version of the story was *Der heilige Abend*), they set out for one of their visits. On their way back, they are surprised by a heavy snowfall. At first they enjoy it, in typical children's fashion, but Konrad soon realizes that he has lost his way. The landmark on top of the mountain ridge, a red post with a memorial tablet, has fallen down and is completely covered by snow. Konrad tries to find another way down to the village after he has given his little sister most of his warm clothing. The children walk with the perseverance and strength only children and animals possess, not knowing that their supply might ever be exhausted. Like the boy in *Granit,* Konrad is endowed, beyond his age, with the instincts and knowledge of children in close contact with nature; he knows what to do and would have brought Sanna back safely if they had not come to a glacier. The glacier scenes are at the center of the story and furnish the main contrast, the children being like tiny wandering dots among its huge stones and ice blocks.

As if driven by instinct to find shelter, they find their way into a glacial cave. It is warm in there, but the eerie blue frightens them, and they leave the cave again. Finally, they find shelter in a "little house," formed accidentally by some big boulders and some great wide slabs on top. It is open in front and dry inside, since the snow has fallen straight down and has not drifted in. And while in the villages there are lights, presents, and joy, the children sit alone in their little cave, huddled close against each other, seeing nothing but the pale snow and the dark sky outside. The most precious presents they were going to receive, the grandparents', lie sealed in the boy's satchel, in the back of the cave. The snow clouds disappear, and a magnificent starry sky opens in front of the children. The children have eaten all the food the grandmother had given them, but they are very tired now after their almost superhuman effort to climb over the glacier, and Sanna falls asleep. The boy

knows of the danger of freezing to death; he remembers the coffee
extract the grandmother had wanted him to take to their mother
and what she had said about it.

After the effect of the coffee has worn off, nature comes to their
help. First, three times, the thundering noise of the cracking ice,
and then a beautiful aurora borealis, a brightly shining arc, extend-
ing through the starry sky and pouring out streams of light, keeps
them awake. The children are so overawed that they do not even
speak to each other. Finally, the sun rises and the children try again
to find their way down. At first, they meet nothing but ice; then,
after they have worked their way out of the glacier, nothing but
snow. But a rescue party finally finds them. Mother and father are
overcome by emotion, and the father, who wants to thank the
searchers, can only say, "Neighbors, friends, I thank you." As they
return to the village, the bell of Christmas Mass rings and they
all fall to their knees to pray. In the evening, the candles of the
Christmas tree are lighted, and the children receive their belated
presents. Sanna, who, with a child's unspoiled sense for wondrous
beauty, had been overwhelmed by the splendor of the aurora borealis, tells her mother that she has seen Christ on the mountain.
From that day on, the children are no longer considered as outsiders, belonging half to Millsdorf, but as natives of Gschaid. The
mother has also become a native of the village.

The beauty of the story lies in the simple blending—without any
miracle—of the events with the Christmas spirit, in Konrad's steadfast courage and concern for his little sister, her unabating trust in
him, and the unforgettable nature scenes. Thanks to Stifter's gift
for putting visual impressions into words, we actually see the mani-
fold shapes of the ice and the boulders, some covered with snow,
reaching out like monstrous paws (III, 217). We vicariously experience with the children the long starry night, from dusk to dawn,
the aurora borealis, the spectacular sunrise—all of it sketched with
the most subtle nuances of light and colors. The descriptions are
enhanced by the immense stillness, possible only so high above
all life.

The English reader is fortunate in having, in the translation by
Elizabeth Mayer and Marianne Moore, a rendering of the story
which, according to W. H. Auden, "reads like an original."[20]

Katzensilber (Mica) is the only story which had not been published elsewhere before it appeared in *Bunte Steine*. It is an appealing tale of a shy, dark-skinned girl *(das braune Mädchen)*, probably a Gypsy, who lives in the woods and makes friends with the children of a conventional family, only to disappear at the end of the story as mysteriously as she had come in the beginning. The family spends the winter in town, and the rest of the year on the paternal farm in a hilly part of Upper Austria, the father being another one of Stifter's many gentlemen-farmers. The grandmother, a pious, simple country woman, stays all year round on the farm. It is she who takes care of the three children, Emma, Clementia, and Sigismund, or *Blondköpfchen, Schwarzköpfchen,* and *Braunköpfchen,* as they are called throughout the story. Every year, as soon as it is warm enough, she takes them to the Nussberg, a high hill which got its name from the many hazelnut bushes growing there. The grandmother tells them local legends, one of which concerns a dark-skinned farmer's servant, Sture Mure, whose child *das braune Mädchen* turns out to be at the very end of the story.

It is on the Nussberg that the girl appears, like Goethe's Mignon, clad in colorful boy's clothes. With great psychological insight, Stifter depicts the girl slowly overcoming her shyness, and mutual affection growing up between her and the three children. The children take her for granted without ever being concerned about her origin and her strangeness. The parents try to find out more about her, but "the children never asked" (293). Twice in the story, Stifter provides the girl with an opportunity to prove her love through action: once during a hailstorm on the Nussberg, and once during a raging fire on the farm. With the unfailing instinct of a creature who is still an integral part of nature *("ein Waldgeschöpf"),* the girl recognizes the signs of the approaching hailstorm and rapidly builds a shelter out of faggots. During the fire, the girl "like a squirrel" climbs a vine growing on the wall of the house and brings the little boy, who was locked in, to safety. Stifter is at his best in the descriptions of the hailstorm and the fire. As with the ice storm in *Die Mappe,* he simultaneously sees the immense destructive power and the esthetic grandeur of such catastrophes. After the hailstorm, the child Emma puts it very succinctly: "It was terrifying and almost splendid" (271). The damage wrought by the hail and the fire is very great, but no human being perishes in either. (In the earlier story, *Die Mappe,* some people, although none of the protagonists, lose their lives during the ice storm.) Within two springs, nature restores itself, and in the garden the father lends a helping hand. Emergency quarters are prepared after the fire, and all places in front of the house are immediately cleaned, so that no "dirt and disorder" may offend the eyes.

Dirt and disorder, as we have seen in *Die Narrenburg,* have no lasting place in Stifter's work. How he would have suffered, had he lived in our littered, polluted world! After everything is finished, the house has become even more beautiful and stately than it had ever been. The two catastrophes and the role of rescuer played by the girl bring her closer and closer to the family, and she finally stays with them altogether. She puts on girl's clothes, which, as with Mignon, affect her very being.[21] Nevertheless, their world cannot become hers. When visitors come, she sits by herself in the garden. Once, during a gay party, the parents find the girl alone, weeping, on a sandpile near the house. All she can say when they try to console her and ask her about her own parents are the enigmatic words, "Sture Mure is dead and the high rock is dead." After a violent outburst of emotion, expressing both her deep affection for the family and her despair, she walks away, never to be seen or heard of again.

Of all the tales in *Bunte Steine, Katzensilber,* with its high degree of stylization, points most clearly to Stifter's later works. Lunding discusses it after *Witiko,* not within the framework of *Bunte Steine.* With the exception of the two catastrophes, all the other events are rhythmical repetitions: the change of seasons, the equally balanced arrival and departure of the family, the climbing of the Nussberg with the first warm sun. Each time, the grandmother and the children sit there on the same old hazelnut root. Each time on their way they have to cross the same little brook where small gray fish are gaily swimming and above which blue dragon flies flutter—a refrain with variations which runs through the entire story.[22] Stifter's friend, Louise von Eichendorff, told him that "the deeply poetic monotony" of the story had the same effect on her as the rising and setting of the sun (*Br VII,* 96–97). Other elements of stylization include the constant use of diminutive nouns, the use of the anaphora *sie gingen, es ging, da waren, da war,* and the repetition of a single trivial action in almost identical words.[23] For many readers "the deeply poetic monotony" may be tedious, rather than calming as it was for Louise von Eichendorff. The excessive use of diminutives might be acceptable for the children in the story, reminding us of the fairy tale of *Snow White and the Seven Dwarfs,* but it becomes rather painful when father, mother, and grandmother are called *Blondköpfchen, Schwarzköpfchen,* and *Weissköpfchen.*[24] Another flaw in the story, not noticed by the critics as far as I know, is the improbability of the mother's not first making sure that all three children are safe before turning, calmly and prudently, to fight the fire.

Bergmilch (Aragonite), the last story in *Bunte Steine* (although actually the earliest), deals with an episode from the Wars of Liberation, which also furnish the scene of *Das alte Siegel.* Both stories were first published in 1843, *Bergmilch* with the title *Wirkungen eines weissen Mantels* (Effects of a White Cloak). This war story by Stifter is characteristically pacifistic and conciliatory. The gruesome extinction of a small detachment of French soldiers by the Tyrolese is only recollected. The three fine men in the German castle, the bachelor lord, the steward, and the tutor of the steward's children, although fundamentally good, become chauvinists, especially the lord, who is depicted as a slightly ludicrous swashbuckler. The mother represents the voice of reason and humaneness. She too wishes the enemy to be driven out of the fatherland, but cannot overlook the fact that the wounds inflicted upon the enemy are wounds inflicted upon human beings. Her attitude reminds us of Goethe, who, on March 14, 1830, defending his position during the Wars of Liberation, said to Eckermann that he had never been able to hate the French, although he had thanked God when they were driven out. She is distressed by the fact that rational beings cannot settle their quarrels rationally instead of killing each other. People who have experienced war, Stifter says, realize what a terrible thing it is. They will look upon the one who wantonly started it as a murderer and scourge of mankind *(Verfolger der Menschheit),* even though later deluded epochs will worship him as a hero and demigod. Were it not for the fact that new generations grow up unfamiliar with the horrors of war, Stifter concludes pessimistically, no one would be reckless enough to start another war (III, 346).

Bergmilch, as Lunding has pointed out, is more strictly a *Novelle* than most of Stifter's stories. Action and suspense are stronger than usual, and in the white cloak the story possesses a leitmotif in accordance with Heyse's famous falcon theory.[25] A young warrior in a white cloak enters the castle at night and forces the lord and the steward to lead him to the top of the tower, where he reconnoiters the position of the enemy. Lulu, the young daughter of the steward, admires the courageous young man; and since he speaks German, she cannot regard him as an enemy. He is an Alsatian, and thus forced by his king to fight for the French. Next day, after the French, through his help, have won the victory, the young man returns to apologize (!) for his behavior during the previous night and to explain why he has to fight on the enemy's side. Years later, when Lulu has grown up and the family is peacefully enjoying their afternoon coffee, the young man in the white cloak appears again. He tells the family that he has, in the meantime, been able to fight for the fatherland. Lulu's earlier admiration can now legitimately change to love, and they marry. Out of the white cloak, two little white cloaks are made for their two little boys, symbolizing the transition from war to peace.

The first version of *Bergmilch,* although sketchier than the second, is nevertheless already pacifist in character. Here, the men of the castle have an opportunity to push the young man to his death from the platform of the house. But the steward, a very mild and kind man in this version, refuses to listen to his master and subsequently thanks God every night that his conscience does not have to carry the burden of murder. In the introductory remarks of the first version, moreover, the "hero" worship of young girls is examined critically, and their admiration of the "crude poetry of action" contrasted with the respect of mature women for the less spectacular feats of the real contributors to the welfare of mankind. This reevaluation of hero worship occurs more than once in Stifter. The pacifist impact of the story, however, suffers from the fact that the hero fights unwillingly on the enemy's side, and in the version of *Bunte Steine,* only temporarily so. Ernst Penzoldt, a modern humanist, pacifist, and great admirer of Stifter, has in many of his stories strengthened the motif of love between enemies by having the two lovers belong to genuinely opposed sides.[26] For this, Stifter was not yet ready.

In the immediate public reception of *Bunte Steine,* positive and negative voices were heard. Of private praise, that which compared

the book with some beautiful illustrations for the *Odyssey,* calling
it simple but great and profound in its effect, and that which attri-
buted to it the clarity and simplicity of Xenophon, must have pleased
Stifter most.[27] Actually, neither *Studien* nor *Bunte Steine* should
be judged collectively. The first version of *Granit (Die Pechbrenner)*
and the *Bunte Steine* versions of *Kalkstein* and *Bergkristall* measure
up to the best of the *Studien;* only parts of the other stories reach
the same heights. One may also object to Stifter's picturing in *all*
the stories only "good," obedient children. When Stifter gave a
copy of *Bunte Steine* to his foster daughter Juliana on her twelfth
birthday, he could easily write on the flyleaf: "Be good like the
children in this book" (*Br II,* 137). The only naughtiness in the
whole book, that in *Granit,* is involuntary, and the only disobe-
dience, that in *Die Pechbrenner,* is caused by compassion. Yet
the most interesting children are the ones who deviate from the
norm: *das braune Mädchen* in *Katzensilber* and the retarded girl
in *Turmalin.* Hein, in another connection, suggests that Stifter,
being childless, did not know children well. But this suggestion has
been refuted.[28] To use it as an explanation for his one-sided charac-
terization of children oversimplifies matters. The emphasis on the
lovable traits in children: innocence, trust, mutual affection, unquestioning obedience; the suppression of other traits, equally
present in reality: mischievousness, assertion of one's will to the
point of stubbornness, fights among siblings—the emphasis and
the suppression are both rooted in Stifter's moral tendency.
"Naughty" children would be the equivalent of "wicked" adults,
so conspicuously absent in Stifter's work. If one compares with
Stifter's idealized figures some other, much more "realistic"—
though still very lovable—children in the writings of *Poetic Realism,* for example, Keller's self-portrait in *Der grüne Heinrich,*
Gotthelf's Bubi in *Käthi die Grossmutter,* Rosegger's largely autobiographical Waldbauernbübel in *Waldheimat,* one realizes once
more how vague, almost meaningless, the literary term *Poetic
Realism* may become.

CHAPTER 5

Der Nachsommer

THERE are few works in the history of literature which, like *Der Nachsommer* (Indian Summer), have received the utmost praise from some and the most annihilating criticism from others. At one extreme there is Hebbel, who declared that he could, without any risk, promise the Polish crown to the reader who finished the book of his own accord. Later Hebbel called it nothing but an encyclopedia.[1] At the other extreme there is Nietzsche's statement that *Der Nachsommer*, together with Goethe's *Conversations with Eckermann*, Lichtenberg's *Aphorisms*, the first book of Jung-Stilling's *Autobiography*, and Gottfried Keller's *Leute von Seldwyla*, is one of the few German prose works which deserve to be read again and again.[2] One modern critic calls it "the greatest of totally unread novels."[3] What admirers of *Der Nachsommer* share is the consciousness of having come upon something unique. They all feel as if they had been drawn into a magic circle, into a realm of timeless beauty where one breathes a different air. In his epilogue to *Der Nachsommer*, Hugo von Hofmannsthal speaks of the "everyday atmosphere" to which the reader must return after finishing the book. Oskar Loerke, in his diary, tells us that he felt paralyzed, so strong was the ecstasy he experienced through "this silence of nature, of things, of man in their final, perfect beauty."[4] Benno Reifenberg, in a diary kept from August to December, 1947, describes his sensations on reading *Der Nachsommer* against the background of torn and devastated Germany. He had to overcome a certain resistance, but he too was drawn more and more into the quiet magic of the novel, "the invincible radiance of the humane" *(in den mächtigen Glanz des Humanen)*.[5] Neither he nor Loerke was ashamed of the tears the book called forth. The author of this study, too, still remembers the supreme enchantment she felt when she read the book for the first time in the quiet of an Alpine village. Even the hero of the novel, after his first visit to the *Rosenhaus*, the main scene of action, feels as if he had come upon a fairy-tale world (IV, 186, 218).

The uniqueness of the work, however, makes it very hard to discuss in a short critical study. How can one convey in a few pages "the final, perfect beauty" of this novel, which has no plot to speak of? Herbert Cysarz claims that one could summarize it in one sentence: "A very carefully and austerely *(hochnotpeinlich)* educated young scientist comes to the house of a certain Von Risach, hears him tell about his youthful love for Mathilde and marries her daughter Natalie."[6] This is, of course, exaggerated simplification, but actually not much more of what we ordinarily call action takes place. To call the novel an *Entwicklungsroman* or *Bildungsroman* and analyze it in comparison with Goethe's *Wilhelm Meister,* or Keller's *Der grüne Heinrich,* or Gotthelf's *Wie Uli der Knecht glücklich ward* and *Uli der Pächter,* is not very helpful either. In contrast to these novels, there is no abundance of interesting minor characters in *Der Nachsommer,* and there are no colorful descriptions of segments of contemporary society. But more important is the fact that the education of the hero is not one of trial, error, and guilt. Although he constantly gains in knowledge, insight, and understanding, he is, as Victor Lange rightly remarks, mature and discerning from the very beginning of the narrative.[7] Were he not, he could not give such a clear picture of the *Nachsommer* world and its protagonists. He has no faults to overcome. He is educated through heightened understanding of nature, art, human relations, and his ever deepening love for Natalie. All this is furthered by the older and wiser man, Risach. But even Risach is more of an observer than a guide, a man who provides the opportunity for development and generously shares his wisdom and experience with the younger man, remaining, however, wary of any direct, premature interference. When, at the very end of the novel, the hero's father praises Risach for having formed and ennobled *(gebildet und veredelt)* his son, Risach disclaims the praise by saying, "He himself *(sein Selbst)* has developed, and all intimate associations which he has enjoyed, yours above all, have helped" (837). His is, to use Goethe's immortal verse the "geprägte Form, die lebend sich entwickelt" (innate form which develops through living). Very similar expressions are used to describe Natalie's development (820). There is some question whether the two young people, Heinrich and Natalie, are the central figures of the novel. Stifter himself denied it in calling them a bright *(heiter)* ornament of the work, whose center of gravity lay elsewhere *(Br III,*

22). In another letter to Heckenast, he makes a strong point of the greatness and wisdom of Risach, who, after an active and influential career as statesman, forms and uplifts everybody around him in the solitude he has chosen (*Br II, 331*). Hofmannsthal feels that *Der Nachsommer* achieves its special eminence, not through the one who is educated but through the one who educates.[8]

Heinrich's development takes place at a leisurely pace. The impressions he receives work long and subconsciously before the results become apparent, as with poets in their seemingly unproductive periods. Stifter, to be sure, emphasizes the value of time as something to be used wisely and never to be squandered. The demands of the day (Goethe's *"die Forderung des Tages"*) must always be fulfilled first (478–79, 703). This principle of regularity and order in one's daily occupations is one of the mainstays in the education of all the young people in the novel (5, 73, 222, 807). But there must also be time simply for living, for cultivated leisure, Romanticism's *"edler Müssiggang,"* something which modern man has almost forgotten. Risach advises his young friend to give up his scientific endeavors for a while, to live first in the city and then on his country estate, without a special purpose, doing whatever the moment and his inclination impel him to do, enjoying the house and the garden, visiting neighbors, and letting things happen as they will (349).

The same slow pace which characterizes Heinrich's development prevails in all human relationships in the novel. Rilke called it *"eines der unbeeiltesten, gleichmässigsten und gleichmütigsten Bücher der Welt"* (one of the most unhurried, harmonious, tranquil books in the world).[9] Nobody thrusts himself upon other people, nobody forces himself into another's confidence, no allusions are made to new situations which have developed, as for instance Heinrich's and Natalie's engagement, and no questions are asked, natural as they might sometimes be. The phrases, "I did not ask" and "I was not asked," occur repeatedly throughout the novel. This is partly a matter of good breeding, a last remnant of the chivalric code of behavior, epitomized in Gurnemanz's admonition to Parzival: Thou shalt not ask too many questions.

But there is more than good manners to this lack of curiosity in *Der Nachsommer,* which does not even ask for the names of host and guest. The name of the hero, Heinrich Drendorf, is not revealed until the very end of the novel (813) and Natalie's family name

not much earlier (803). The names are accidental and have nothing
to do with the essence of a person. In this patient refraining from
asking questions, in the great respect for another's privacy, there
is expressed an infinite trust in the other person, and also an implicit trust that everything will come out right in the end.

Risach, in one of the numerous conversations about art, gives
us the key words of the whole novel: *Ergebung, Vertrauen, Warten*
(resignation, confidence, patience) (453). Important revelations are
never made on the spot; the young people possess a self-control
which seems almost unnatural. When Heinrich and Natalie meet
the day after they have assured each other of their mutual love,
Natalie does not immediately tell Heinrich of her mother's consent,
on which their future happiness depends; it is only after a long
walk and conversation, at the moment of their separation, that
she speaks of it. The most important disclosure, the story of Risach's
and Mathilde's youthful love, is withheld until almost the end of
the novel. After close ties between Heinrich and Natalie have been
established, Risach deems it improper not to unveil the secret of
his relationship to Natalie's mother. But he does not want to do so
until much later, so that Heinrich may, in the meantime, gain the
greatest possible inner calm to receive the communication with full
understanding *(Klarheit)*. But even at that later date, Risach lets
a few days pass before he begins his narration and prefaces it with
many general remarks before, on the next day, he starts the story
proper, "Der Rückblick" (the flashback). Impatient readers will
find such a piling up of delays unbearable, but the novel was not
written for them. Stifter even felt that the effect of the book would
be enhanced in subsequent readings, because then the reader, lifted
above ordinary life and feeling greater and purer as a human being,
would no longer be distracted by the plot—he calls it *"das Stoffliche"*
(Br II, 298). Most readers of *Der Nachsommer* will agree with Stifter's
statement.

The novel is written in the first person, but those who expect out-
bursts of feeling, or constant probing into intimate and subtle moods,
as in Goethe's *Werther* or Stifter's early *Feldblumen,* will be disappointed. Feelings are always restrained and very seldom openly
expressed. The awakening love between Heinrich and Natalie, for
example, must be guessed through gentle intimations: Natalie's
desire to be alone, to take long walks, Heinrich's vague yearnings

and melancholy moods and his sudden interest in Spanish, the language Natalie is studying. The most open indications of their love are Natalie's blushing, their being frightened when they unexpectedly meet, and their inability to find words in each other's presence.

The whole tenor of the book is autumnal, as the title indicates, with all the stillness, serenity, consummate beauty, and gentle melancholy of fall. Autumn is a favorite season in many of Stifter's stories.[10] Several journeys in *Der Nachsommer* are undertaken in that season. The words with which Heinrich summarizes his feelings during a trip into the highland north of the *Rosenhaus* could be used as a motto for the whole novel: "I immersed my soul in the lovely autumn haze which enveloped everything, I let it descend into the deep gorges past which we drove now and then, and surrendered it in profound tranquillity to the peace and stillness which surrounded us" (445). Adjectives like *ruhig* (quiet), *mild, sanft* (gentle), *klar* (clear), *einfach* (simple), *schön* (beautiful), and the corresponding nouns, abound in the book.

The self-possession and serenity of the old people, Risach and Mathilde, color the characters of the young people, Heinrich and Natalie. Natalie's brother Gustav, a handsome youth with all the fascination which this transitional age has for the artist, the lover of beauty, is not young in the ordinary sense of the word: he is too perfect, too quiet, sensible and disciplined. Passion and impatience are restricted to the flashback, the story of Risach and Mathilde, who failed just because they could not wait—one is tempted to say because they were young. Risach was a tutor in Mathilde's home, mainly for Mathilde's younger brother. The young people fell in love, but the parents felt that their love was premature, and the mother asked Risach to tell Mathilde that they should wait. He did so because of his breach of the parents' confidence in him. He also wrongly believed that it would be easier for Mathilde if he himself informed her of the wishes of her parents. But she, still younger than Risach, felt that he had betrayed their love. She argued that she had to obey her parents, but that he was not bound by any filial duty. She broke with him. After Risach had become successful and could marry her, she did not want to be approached by him and let him know that she despised him. Both married without love and lost their respective partners. Much later, after both had passed the prime of life, Mathilde came to Risach to ask his forgiveness for the wrong she had done him. Mathilde had two children (Natalie and Gustav), Risach none. Mathilde bought the *Sternenhof*, an estate not far from Risach's estate, and entrusted her son to the childless man.

A relationship of deep love and friendship has grown up between the two old people, *"das Spiegelklarste ... was menschliche Verhältnisse aufzuweisen haben"* (the purest and most serene of human relationships) (800). They pass their Indian summer in unbroken tranquillity without having experienced a preceding summer. The leitmotif of Indian summer is sounded early in the novel when Risach remarks that even the birds enjoy a carefree Indian summer, as it were, after they have brought up their families and before they migrate (216). Stifter makes certain that Mathilde's and Risach's fate does not befall Heinrich and Natalie. The opposite happens to them—they almost forfeit their happiness by waiting too long and by not declaring their mutual love. Even after the declaration and the consent of all concerned, the marriage has to be postponed for two years, so that Heinrich can undertake a long European journey *(Bildungsreise)*. He wants to be on a par with Natalie, who has already experienced this part of education in earlier extensive travels with her mother.

Der Nachsommer has often been criticized for its length, its elaborations, and its many details. Eight years after its publication, Stifter himself wrote to Heckenast about occasional long passages which must be changed.[11] Whatever one may think of this statement, it is amazing how the first chapter, "Die Häuslichkeit," takes us *in medias res* and how all the main themes are immediately announced. It is like a musical composition, where all the leitmotifs are sounded in the first movement, to be enriched and varied later on.

There is a model family: father, mother, Heinrich and his younger sister Klothilde. At the end of the novel, a new model family is founded. Noble, pure, well-ordered family life seemed to Stifter what his times needed most. The father, a self-made man like Risach, is an industrious merchant of humble origin. He maintains a patriarchal relationship with his clerks, who eat with the family. Risach would like to have all the people in his household eat at his table, but realizes that this is no longer possible. The mother is an exemplary housewife; she is extremely kind and would allow some deviations from the strictly regulated life of the children, but she does not wish to offend the father. This reminds one of the conduct of Goethe's parents.

A spirit of almost pedantic orderliness and cleanliness reigns in the house; thus, Heinrich feels immediately at home in the *Rosenhaus* and the *Sternenhof,* where the same spirit prevails. This spirit is, as we have seen, the trademark of Stifter's writings. Nothing is unimportant, because the inward and the outward aspects correspond. The father does not approve of a multipurpose room any more than he approves of a jack-of-all-trades. That the family can have so many rooms shows, at the outset, the utopian character of the novel. The suburban house into which they move from the town house contains, besides the ordinary rooms, a library, a picture gallery, a room for antique furniture, and another for a collection of old arms. This last room has two glass walls where ivy is growing outside and inside. There is one more room, hung in red silk, whose purpose is as yet undetermined. The house is really a miniature museum and prepares us for the *Rosenhaus.* Heinrich's father has only two collections which outshine those of Risach— his pictures and his cut stones. When we read the list of painters whose pictures he possesses, such as Titian, Dürer, Holbein, Claude Lorrain, Ruysdael, when we find among his cut stones the famous *gemma augustea,* we leave the reality of a wealthy middle-class family far behind.

Life within the family is simple; the education of the children aims at an all-round development of body and mind, as does Gustav's at the *Rosenhaus.* When Heinrich must choose a vocation, he decides, with the consent of his father, to study first the various sciences without regard for any practical use. To the objection that such a procedure is selfish and without utilitarian value, the father, in a very Goethean manner, replies that man exists first for his own sake and not for society's sake. Only by developing his innate abilities can he really be useful to society. These words are repeated almost verbatim when Risach tells Heinrich his life story, regretting that life had granted him only an Indian summer for what he was destined to be. He had become a statesman, although he was meant to be a priest of the beautiful—not as a creative artist, but as a mediator and interpreter of art in insensitive times. In a letter to Louise von Eichendorff, who had complained that she did not fully understand the meaning of the novel, Stifter wrote that the goal of life on earth was often and clearly defined in the book as the full realization of all one's powers in harmonious activity—the way to one's own, and, thus, to other people's, happiness (*Br VII,* 199–200, 206–7, *III,* 124).

When Heinrich is old enough, he spends his summers away from home in order to become thoroughly acquainted with the surrounding countryside, its flora, fauna, minerals, its people, their way of living, and their industries. "Already as a boy," he says, "I had been close to the reality of things as they appear in nature or in the ordered course of human life" (25). During several summers he visits the Alps. Once, on his way from the high mountains to the foothills, he fears being overtaken by a thunderstorm and looks for shelter. A house on a hill, which he has noticed on former journeys, its shimmering white contrasting sharply with the grays and blues of the landscape, looks very inviting. When he approaches, he sees that the front of the house is covered with beautiful roses of many colors, their leaves unharmed by insects.

Although the owner of the house tells him that there will be no thunderstorm, he is invited to stay (the reverse of the situation in *Kalkstein*), and this chance meeting turns out to be the most important event of the novel. Two chapters, "Die Einkehr" and "Die Beherbergung," are devoted to descriptions of the house, its surroundings, its inhabitants, and their occupations. Heinrich's father's love of beauty is here repeated on a grander scale: the reader is overwhelmed by so much perfection. A marble hall and an antique statue on a marble staircase are the climax of all the beauty. The marble hall is a symphony of color and light; the colors of the floor, the ceiling, and the walls are arranged to form a harmonious whole. By day the room receives its light from three large windows, at night from four almost black marble lamps. There is no furniture, but doors of beautiful dark wood are set into three of the walls. The fragrance of roses, entering through the open windows, permeates the whole room.

In the other rooms there are exquisite pieces of furniture, and the son thinks longingly of his father, who would enjoy seeing them. The more Heinrich learns to appreciate art, the more intimate the relationship between him and his father, as well as between him and Risach, becomes. Love of beauty in all its manifestations—

nature, the human body, art, and human relations—is the basic theme of *Der Nachsommer*. "It was written," Stifter remarked, "with Goethe's love of art, conceived and thought out with fervent devotion to quiet, pure beauty" (*Br III,* 93). Thus, it is natural that so many pages of the novel are filled with descriptions of landscapes, houses, furniture, pictures, statues, cut stones, jewelry, and of the restoration of works of art to their original beauty. Risach employs an artist and four workmen to restore old furniture and create new pieces. In addition to these time-consuming occupations, the owner of the *Asperhof* is also a gentleman-farmer who tries to educate his neighbors through his quiet, patient example of model farming. The gardens are in perfect condition. Tree trunks are washed with soap, and thanks to Risach's loving protection of birds on his property, plants are not marred by insects. But this is Utopia: although not a single leaf is eaten, there are still some caterpillars left. After all, what would a garden be without butterflies? Dogs and cats are trained not to go into the garden and harm the birds. Otherwise, they must be given up. Who has ever "educated" a cat except in Utopia!

Stifter's deep reverence for life is akin to Albert Schweitzer's. Heinrich feels profound pity for a stag felled by hunters, and Risach speaks sharply against bird-trapping. Risach's kindness to animals is extended to those that do harm if not watched properly; they are killed only if there is no other way to protect the farm. Flowers can be brought in from the garden only in pots; no cut flowers are allowed in the house. Constant observation of the plants and animals around him, especially the insects, enables Risach to tell Heinrich with certainty that no thunderstorm will occur. A loving, nonanthropocentric attitude, in which, as for God, there exists no *"gross und klein,"* is the prerequisite to such an intimate communion with nature. In this, Risach resembles Gregor in *Der Hochwald.*

Of all the flowers cultivated at the *Asperhof,* the rose is the favorite, and the rose motif, the most important leitmotif in the novel, is sounded again and again. It is the roses in their great profusion and beauty that first catch Heinrich's eye as he approaches the house on the hill. The many varieties of roses at the *Asperhof* are exceptionally well kept. Even fading roses have a beauty of their own, comparable to that of older women, who sometimes show traces of their youthful beauty. In this image, used by Risach (58), the two leitmotifs, that of the rose and that of Indian summer, are blended. When, on a later visit to the *Asperhof*, Heinrich sees Mathilde for the first time, the beauty of the fading rose comes back to his mind.[12] Once, in the middle of the novel, Heinrich overhears by chance a conversation between Mathilde and Risach. Mathilde remarks that their happiness has withered like the roses, whereupon Risach replies that it has not withered, but only taken on another form (427).

In the flashback, we learn that roses had played an important part in their youthful romance.[13] The front of Risach's house, covered with roses, is a repetition, on a larger scale, of the garden pavilion which Mathilde's parents had erected on their country estate. Mathilde's room is shown to Heinrich on his first visit at Risach's house without her name being mentioned. The green carpet and the rose-colored silk tapestry on the walls evoke in him the image of a lawn bordered by overhanging roses. He calls it the *"Rosenzim-merchen"* (little rose room), just as he calls the house the *"Rosen-haus,"* since he does not like the name *"Asperhof."* The shimmer of the roses is the last thing he can distinguish when he turns around once more on his way back to the mountains after his first visit. The halcyon days of the season of blooming roses add to the peace-fulness of the landscape in which the *Rosenhaus* is situated. Sounds like the chirping of the crickets, the humming of bees, the singing of birds in the garden, are felt by Heinrich to be "a different kind of stillness" (64) or "as almost a stillness" (129). Many of Heinrich's later visits take place in the same season of flowering roses. The calendar of the novel is determined by the roses, so to speak. Their burgeoning, the height of their bloom, their withering, the loving care lavished on them in winter, are always noted. The peak of their beauty is celebrated as a holiday to which neighbors and friends are invited. At the very end of the novel, after the wedding, the high point of their bloom is celebrated by the united families as a com-memoration which looks to the future as well as to the past.[14]

After Heinrich's first stay at the *Rosenhaus*, renewed visits there alternate rhythmically with sojourns at his own home and at the *Sternenhof*, and with scientific journeys to the Alps. To avoid the monotony of a too regular pattern, many little trips are inserted: to the *Inghof*, where friends of Risach and Mathilde live, to the father's native region, to the highland north of the *Asperhof*, to

Gothic churches and altars. The trips are undertaken in various combinations: by Heinrich alone, in the company of his father or his sister, or together with his new friends. No visit to any of the places mentioned is an exact repetition of the previous one; each varies in length, season, and importance. What they have in common is the fact that all contribute to Heinrich's development. Heinrich's growth occurs in concentric circles; the circles enlarge as Heinrich makes new discoveries and as his human ties become closer. In a letter to Heckenast, Stifter compared the organization *(Haushalt)* of the book to the growth of a tree, where the seed has to be planted, so that later the leaves, blossoms, and finally the fruit may come, blossoms and fruit being here *"wärmere Gefühle und tiefere Handlungen"* (warmer affections and more significant actions) (*Br II,* 298). This organization is also expressed in the first three chapter headings of the second volume: "Die Erweiterung," "Die Annäherung," "Der Einblick" (Widening, Rapprochement, Insight).

The matchless beauty of the *Rosenhaus* and its works of art, the seriousness with which conversations about art and artistic endeavors are pursued there, open Heinrich's eyes. Although his natural bent is scientific, he pays more and more attention to art and in his drawings changes from a purely objective to a more artistic approach. The turning point in the novel occurs when Heinrich, who had often seen the Greek marble statue on the staircase, suddenly perceives its incomparable beauty. A deep, universal human feeling, that is, his slowly ripening love for Natalie, has been the catalyst. It is a revelation in the proper sense of the word, and the lightning which illuminates the statue in roseate light may be taken as an outward symbol of the inner enlightenment. Strangely enough, the relatively late Greek model for the statue, although beautiful, is somewhat disappointing for people who have known it first through Stifter's description.[15]

After this turning point in Heinrich's development, his friends can indulge in conversations about art which they have previously avoided out of consideration for him. This awakening changes the relationship between Heinrich and his father. Mutual respect is added to the natural bond of affection; in one of the most moving scenes in the novel, Heinrich realizes that his father is not an ordinary merchant, but a remarkable man of profound culture who possesses works of art no less valuable and beautiful than Risach's. The father knows that he can now share his greatest joys with his son.

Love of beauty is intrinsic to all the characters in the novel; life and art are inextricably interwoven. "The conversations about art and life are . . . expressions of the characters of Risach, the merchant, Mathilde, and the merchant's wife; through them the fine young people[16] in the book are educated to a certain level" (*Br III,* 95). The highest praise Heinrich can find for Natalie's features is that they resemble the features of antique cameos, sharing their ingenuous, lofty, simple, delicate, and yet strong character, suggesting a perfect body, but also an independent will and soul. Her classic beauty prevents easy intimacy with her, as is shown when Heinrich's father sees her for the first time (811). The marble statue becomes dearer and dearer to Heinrich after he knows that there exists a living being akin to it. The marble statue, Homer's Nausikaa, and Natalie blend into one figure for him (702–3). Louise von Eichendorff sensed a slightly pagan, anti-Christian tone in the novel and found the contrast to the works of her brother more definite here than in any other writing of Stifter (*Br VII,* 200). The word "anti-Christian" seems too strong, but, on the whole, her judgment was astute. *Der Nachsommer* is Stifter's hymn to antiquity. More than any other figures of Stifter, Natalie and Gustav are incarnations of the Greek ideal of Kalokagathia, the fusion of the beautiful and the good.[17] If Ernst Penzoldt has been called an "Attic Protestant" by his friend Erich Kästner, one might justly call Stifter an "Attic Catholic."[18]

Heinrich's ever-deepening insight into art and his progress in drawing and painting are followed in great detail. His work, as well as Gustav's timid beginnings, are judged by the experts. Music, however, plays an astonishingly small role in the novel as compared to the visual arts. Heinrich, Klotilde, Mathilde, and Natalie play the zither, although Heinrich himself once remarks that this instrument belongs exclusively to the mountains. Joseph, the great zither player, is a hunter in the mountains, a perpetual wanderer, and does not belong at all to the settled, aristocratic *Nachsommer* world. The minor role of music adds to the impression of stillness, perhaps the foremost characteristic of the novel. To become even more aware of this stillness, one has only to compare *Der Nachsommer* with Eichendorff's narrative prose—for example, with his famous story, *Aus dem Leben eines Taugenichts,* where the air constantly vibrates with the sounds of twittering and singing birds, of instruments and songs.

An important part of Heinrich's education is his growing understanding of poetry. Only at the beginning of the novel, while perusing
a small bookshelf at the *Rosenhaus,* can he make the deprecating
remark that it contains almost nothing but poetry. Of all his encounters with great poetry, however, only one is reported at length: his
attendance at a performance of *King Lear* with a famous actor in
the title role. The name of the actor is not mentioned, but we know
that it was Anschütz, whom Stifter had seen in the Vienna Burg-
theater.[19] We experience Heinrich's reactions vicariously. Since he
had not read the play, we follow the course of the action with him
as it unfolds on the stage. Reduced to essentials, the action is narrated in simple but poignant terms. Heinrich bestows the highest
praise possible for Stifter on the play: *"wirklichste Wirklichkeit"*
(197), which literally means "most real reality," but which probably
should be rendered in English as "highest truth."

Heinrich is shaken to the very depth of his being and knows that
the happy ending which his age contrived cannot be true. After his
emotion has somewhat subsided, his glance falls upon an "indescribably beautiful" girl, who is also overcome by deep emotion.
As they leave the theater, their eyes meet for a second in brief ac-
knowledgment, as it were, of their spiritual affinity. Heinrich does
not recognize her as the girl he had seen on his first departure from
the *Rosenhaus,* but the leitmotif for Natalie is sounded again, that
is, his thought that the human face is probably the most fitting object for drawing (178, 200, 311). When he becomes acquainted with
Natalie later on, he has the feeling that he has seen her before,
but cannot remember where. Natalie, on the other hand, immediately
recognizes him, but does not tell him until much later, at the time
of their engagement, thus confirming, once more, their spiritual kinship. Since both Heinrich and Natalie are usually calm, poised and
self-possessed, their emotion roused by a great work of art is all
the more striking. Only twice in the novel—here, and in the flashback—are such strong emotions shown.

In his systematic way, Heinrich now sets out to read Shakespeare's
works in the original. Ever-widening acquaintance with great poets
enriches his personality. His tendency toward a certain scientific
dryness and soberness is counterbalanced by his communion with
poets; their words produce in him a vague longing for a future which
he cannot as yet precisely define. When Heinrich tells him of his

new inner experience, Risach calls poets the greatest benefactors of mankind. For him, they are priests of the beautiful, who, amid all the change of views concerning the world, man, and even God, convey to us that which is eternally human and will always delight us *(das allzeit Beglückende)* (343). Nothing could be further removed from modern esthetics than the thought that the transmission of beauty, joy, and deep happiness is the foremost task of literature. Heinrich's favorite writers are the Greeks, whose works he carries with him on almost all his trips. They seem to him more natural, truer, simpler, and greater than the moderns. Of later periods, only the *Nibelungenlied* and Calderón are mentioned; of contemporary writers none. If, on each visit to the main scenes of the novel, Heinrich sees his scientific and artistic pursuits in better perspective, his human ties are strengthened too. There are numerous hints, mainly through meticulous catering to any possible need he may have, that on each subsequent visit he is a more and more welcome guest at the *Rosenhaus* and the *Sternenhof*. Thoughtful hospitality and well-chosen gifts are here, as in many other works of Stifter, symbols of the love and consideration people have for one another—people who are hesitant to express their feelings in words.

The central relationship in the novel, that between Heinrich and Natalie, is almost wordless up to the time of their engagement. Even afterward few conversations take place between them, and no letters are exchanged. In many ways, however, their silences are more eloquent than any conversation could be. What conversations there are appear stilted at times. When the two lovers exchange their vows, they use the intimate *"du,"* but they return immediately to the more formal *"Ihr,"* and the next day, Heinrich addresses Natalie once with *"Fräulein,"* the most formal address. Their whole conversation on the second day appears somewhat strained and pedantic for two young people who have just discovered that their love is mutual. Modern critics have found fault with the great restraint in the relationship between the two lovers and their complete submission to the will of their elders. Thus, one critic speaks of the pale spring of their love.[20] It is true that Stifter's didactic purpose, that is, the conscious contrast with Risach's and Mathilde's story, tones down the relationship between Heinrich and Natalie. But their restraint is in keeping with the whole tenor of the book. Present-day readers might welcome this absence of "sex" as a respite from an overdose of it in contemporary literature. What makes Heinrich and Natalie so different from young lovers in other literary works is their close communion with nature, and their being always at one with themselves. Even when she thinks her love unrequited, Natalie can say, referring to her long, lonely walks: "And the still-ness then gives peace to one's soul and will" (505). One cannot help feeling that neither of them would have been completely unhappy without the crowning experience of their union. Their love is very deep, because neither has ever flirted, and they have kept the secret of it to themselves without impairing the strength of their feelings through premature talk. One may object to so much perfection in human beings, especially in young people, but one cannot read *Der Nachsommer* as a "realistic" novel. One has to read it as Stifter intended it and explained it in a letter to Heckenast:

I wanted to depict a profounder and richer life in this work than occurs ordinarily, perfected and open to our view in Risach and Mathilde, partial and more one-sided, in the merchant and his wife, and slightly visible even in Eustach and the gardener: a life developing and maturing in the young scientist, in Natalie, Roland, Klotilde, Gustav, through association with the already perfected lives. . . . Ordinary life, but not really a life in humble circumstances, is sketched in the *Inghof,* the parties in the city . . . and the visitors at the *Sternenhof. (Br III,* 94)

The maturing of the young people takes place without any rebellion on their part, without any friction between the generations. There is no generation gap, because the young people can identify with the ideals of their elders. They have no difficulty in growing up to them, because they are *"edel,"* that is, of a noble disposition. They are like *les gens bien nés* (the wellborn people) of Rabelais's famous Abbey Thelema, who are naturally drawn toward virtue and re-pelled by vice.[21] Or, as Stifter states in somewhat similar terms at the very beginning of the novel, "God gave the practice of virtue a particular charm and beauty after which noble minds strive" (16). The young people become what they are mainly through spending their time in the company of older persons, listening to their con-versations. For Stifter, genuine education is possible only through association with greater and more mature minds *("Erziehung ist wohl nichts als Umgang").* (741)

None of the main characters of the novel has anything odd about him; none withdraws from society. Yet, in encounters with outsiders at the *Sternenhof* or in the city, great care is taken to show that they are all of a higher type. The mark of their nobility is their naturalness and their simplicity, especially in their way of dressing. They never have any desire to show off or to appear brilliant. The young people scarcely take part in conversations; when at a neighbor's house Natalie is asked to play the piano, she quietly refuses. She never shows her embroidery and never plays on the zither for others, and neither does her mother. Their being so different prevents the young people from having any real friends outside their own small circle. One exception seems to be Heinrich's friendship with the young jeweler in town, but this is based exclusively on their common artistic interests. Natalie and Klotilde have no "girl friends," and Gustav has no friend before he meets Heinrich, who is, after all, a few years his senior. All the main characters are what human beings could be under ideal conditions; this precludes any real individualization.

The most impressive character is Risach, who possesses the proverbial wisdom, kindness, and serenity of old age, whose sphere of activity is large enough to allow him to realize all his formerly unfulfilled dreams. He has reached the stage where the voices of our own desires are no longer so loud that *"die Unschuld der Dinge"* (innocence of objects) cannot penetrate to us (218–19). Mathilde is the incarnation of the grace, calm and resignation we should acquire with advancing years. She *is* what Wilhelm von Humboldt wanted the woman to whom he addressed his *Briefe an eine Freundin* to be.[22] Heinrich's parents represent a model marriage and model parents. Heinrich is a model son and brother, and Klotilde a model daughter and sister. Gustav is an exemplary youth, Eustach an exemplary artisan, Simon a model gardener, and Katherina a model housekeeper.

So much perfection would be unbearable without the human failings shown in the flashback and some hints at the dangerous depths in human nature as revealed in the only two real artists in the novel—the vagabond zither player Joseph, and especially Eustach's brother Roland. One could wish that Stifter had given them a larger role. All we know of Roland's work is one huge, very unusual landscape painting, which shows great promise. Risach recognizes "the problem of the artist" in Roland, but in keeping with the optimistic tenor of the whole novel, he hopes that he can straighten things out by sending the young man off to Rome.[23] One human conflict the modern reader will perceive in the novel, and which is arising out of Klotilde's fixation on her brother, seems to be resolved too optimistically. It is assumed that Klotilde will love Natalie like a sister without a trace of jealousy. Because of this lack of individualization and human failings, I seriously doubt that the reader can identify himself with any of the characters. But it is exactly this "pure" ideality that makes *Der Nachsommer* the unique work it is.

Again, as in all his works, Stifter in *Der Nachsommer* does not portray the appearance of his characters in any detail; he merely suggests, setting our imagination to work. When Heinrich sees Natalie for the first time, nothing is said about her features except that he thinks that the human face may be the most beautiful object for drawing. Later on in the novel, he uses such general terms as "indescribably," "infinitely," "extraordinarily" beautiful to describe the indelible impression she makes upon him, and once we get a glimpse of "a beautiful hand" feeding the birds, which he recognizes as hers.

As far as actual description goes, Stifter limits himself almost exclusively to the colors of hair and eyes, which, as in *Brigitta, Abdias, Kalkstein,* serve also as leitmotifs. Natalie and Gustav have brown hair and dark eyes, which they have inherited from their mother, and which thus form a link between the novel proper and the flashback. Risach's white hair, which he keeps uncovered even in bad weather, is mentioned again and again, most strikingly where the sleet mingles with its whiteness (686). What makes Stifter's descriptions so suggestive is the fact that the inward and the outward are interwoven. A mouth is called "dear and beautiful" or "lovely *(hold)* and unspeakably kind" (241–42). When Natalie, for the third time, evokes in Heinrich the thought that the human face is the most worthwhile subject for drawing, he says, *"so süss gehen ihre reinen Augen und so lieb und hold gehen ihre Züge in die Seele des Betrachters"* (Her clear eyes enter so sweetly, and her features so dearly and charmingly, into the soul of the onlooker) (311)[24]. In the repeated comparison of Mathilde with a fading rose, there is as much recollection of her former beauty as of the grace with which she has grown old. Her beauty reflects her soul, which is so kind and composed now and thus affects the people around her. Natalie's affinity with the marble statue, her and Gustav's affinity with the antique cameos, reveal as much of their particular type of beauty as of their whole being. When Stifter compares Natalie with two other "enchanting" girls, what could describe her beauty better than the felicitous phrase, *"aber um Natalie war etwas wie ein tiefes Glück verbreitet"* (but around Natalie, there was something like an aura of deep happiness)? (263)

Special attention is given to the way people dress: the color, cut, and material of their costumes are almost always indicated. Stifter may have felt that these are matters which the reader can visualize more easily than facial features, but each of these details also has a special significance. Risach's going bareheaded indicates a vigor unusual in a man of his age; the gardener's white clothing, which, together with his white hair, makes him just "the white gardener" (130), sets him apart from the men in Eustach's workshop, who wear big green aprons. It denotes in him—the very old man—purity, dignity, and social status. His wife is also dressed in white. That white is the most impractical color imaginable for a gardener does not matter at all! Risach's strange and extremely simple way of dressing makes Heinrich first mistake him for a steward—an echo of a scene from *Brigitta*. But soon Heinrich begins to admire the man in spite of his peculiar and almost absurd costume, and on his second visit, he becomes so accustomed to it that it no longer irritates him. He increasingly feels that this dress is best suited to Risach's home and the people living near him; it differentiates him from them without placing him above them. It also seems to Heinrich in better taste than the dress of city people. Stifter has Risach, Mathilde, Natalie, and Gustav dress more or less differently from other members of their class (the men more so than the women), to show their superiority. The proverb *"Kleider machen Leute"* (fine feathers make fine birds) is here used in reverse. It is the great naturalness and simplicity of their clothes which bring into sharp focus natural beauty and human greatness. A visit from neighboring friends makes Heinrich fully aware of this circumstance:

Their ornate attire seemed to me showy and unnatural, whereas the other was simple and appropriate. It looked as if Mathilde, Natalie, my old host, and even Gustav were remarkable people, whereas the others were members of a crowd that one might find anywhere. (262)

The great attention Stifter pays to clothing is also due to his predominantly visual imagination. He sees the figures as they walk, sit, and stand, and with a few masterstrokes can make us see them too. A good example of this is the scene on the morning after the engagement when Heinrich happens to watch Natalie for a brief moment. She stands almost in the middle of a room, into which Heinrich looks through a half-open glass door. Some exquisite medieval cupboards form the backdrop; in front of her is a table, covered with an ornate antique tablecloth, on which two zithers lie. She wears a light gray dress with fine red stripes, which flows in rich folds from her hips to the floor. Like all of Natalie's dresses, it closes with a high, plain neckline, and its narrow sleeves are trimmed at the wrists with a darker ribbon, looking like a bracelet. She stands erect, the upper part of her body bending slightly backward. Her left arm is outstretched, and the hand rests on a book standing upright on the table. Her right hand rests lightly on her lower left arm. Her indescribably beautiful face is at peace.

What distinguishes this verbal painting from an actual painting is Heinrich's interpretation, what he adds to the visual impression: "Such a pure, delicate spirituality showed in her features, as I had never seen before in her who always revealed her innermost being. I also understood what her figure expressed. I heard her say to herself, as it were, 'It has come to pass!' " (584). It is always dangerous to liken figures in fiction to actual paintings, but Natalie's classical features bring to this author's mind Anselm Feuerbach's *Nana.* One might even call Natalie a less austere, slightly gentler version of *Nana.* Benno Reifenberg also feels that Feuerbach could have painted such scenes as the party at the *Sternenhof,* with people in festive clothes walking in the park and a marble nymph in an ivy-clad grotto.[25]

As in any *Bildungsroman,* the question arises as to how much of *Der Nachsommer* is autobiographical. Since the novel is, to such a large extent, utopian, it cannot be strictly autobiographical. It does not retell Stifter's actual life, as, for instance, Keller's *Der grüne Heinrich* narrates, in a large measure, Keller's own life. However, many of Stifter's experiences are woven into the novel. All the scenes in city and countryside were familiar to Stifter. Risach's childhood and early youth resemble Stifter's in all important details (723–26); both studied law and science in Vienna; both earned their bread as private tutors; both experienced in their youth a great love which did not find fulfillment. When Risach tries to explain to Heinrich the essence of his being, which is that of an artist, a lover of form *(Gestalt)* and beauty, we hear Stifter speak. We hear him again when Risach, who was so successful as a statesman, maintains, nevertheless, that he was not fit for this profession. He did not want to do what was merely expedient, but rather, with his *"Ehrfurcht vor den Dingen, wie sie an sich sind"* (respect for things as they are in themselves),[26] find permanent solutions based upon the intrinsic nature of situations (718–19). Beyond this inner kinship between Risach and Stifter, *Der Nachsommer* embodies all of Stifter's interests, serious endeavors, and hobbies. It is, in a sense, the sum total of his life. With Heinrich, Stifter shares scientific interests and many attempts at landscape painting. With Risach, he shares a concern for saving medieval art from decay, joy in collecting and restoring old furniture, and a deep-seated pedagogical bent. With the gardener, he shares a great love of cacti.

Many objects and incidents in the novel are taken directly from Stifter's life. The three most precious pieces of furniture—the writing table with the dolphin feet, the wardrobe so delicately inlaid, and the table with its design of musical instruments—were all in Stifter's possession. The Kefermarkt Altar, in the restoration of which Stifter played such an important part, appears in the novel as the Kerberg Altar.[27] Stifter's friend, Amélie von Handel, describes how he called her and her husband in the middle of the night to watch with him the unfolding of a rare cactus blossom, enhanced by surrounding lights.[28] In the novel, the gardener Simon has the great joy of showing his employer and his friends the delicate blossom of the *cereus peruvianus* on Heinrich's and Natalie's wedding day. Heinrich, Natalie, and Klotilde go a second time at night to admire it, surrounded by lamps.

In many figures of the novel we can easily recognize friends and acquaintances of Stifter whom he thus immortalized: in the princess, the Princess Anna Maria von Schwarzenberg; in her companion and reader, the poetess Betty Paoli. In Heinrich we find traits of the Alpine researcher Simony. Heinrich's jeweler friend in the city is Stifter's close friend Joseph Türck. How much Freiherr Andreas von Baumgartner, Stifter's teacher and patron in Vienna, contributed to the figure of Risach, remains controversial.[29] Nowhere in the novel are actual names given. This is quite understandable in the case of personal friends, but why are the names of the emperor and of the famous actor in the performance of *King Lear* withheld? Stifter wanted to give the novel a "timeless" quality.

In a letter to Heckenast, written in 1857, Stifter asks him to change the subtitle of his work from "A Narration of Our Times" to "A Narration," with the significant addition: "The reader himself must find out the time" (*Br III,* 14). Actually, the reader of *Der Nachsommer* will hardly be curious about the specific historical setting. We know from the same letter to Heckenast that the time is the *Vormärz,* that is, the time before the 1848 Revolution. Stifter says more specifically that the narration "takes place not in our time, but over thirty years ago." At one point in the novel, however, Risach (that is, Stifter) has a prophetic vision of the revolution which the rapid advancement of science and technology will effect. He sees the inherent danger for mankind. But, in accordance with his generally optimistic view of history as advancing toward the good, he believes that the human mind will finally manage to regain control over the forces it has unleashed and reach hitherto unknown heights (535–37).

In spite of all the identifications we have listed, one cannot call *Der Nachsommer* an autobiographical novel. It is rather the strongest expression of the ideal life of which Stifter had dreamed since his early *Feldblumen.* The term a modern critic uses for it, "the novel of extended dream," seems well chosen.[30] It is a dream of a life of leisure and self-fulfillment, unhampered by material worries and the fetters of a profession; a life spent in beautiful surroundings in the company of congenial friends. *Der Nachsommer* receives a great deal of its luster and beauty through contrast with the life Stifter led while he wrote it. During those years, complaints about his official duties abound in his letters and become increasingly bitter. After the publication of the novel, he gave his dream of the ideal life the name *"Nachsommer";* he even invented the word *"Nachsommerer,"* meaning people spending their *"Nachsommer"* together.[31] His dream found its realization only in the novel. When he wrote to Heckenast two months after being pensioned, "My Indian summer has started," this proved to be a tragic illusion (*Br V,* 131). He never had his Indian summer, nor did he ever achieve the serenity and composure of Risach's and Mathilde's old age.

In recent years, two new attacks have been leveled at *Der Nach-sommer* for not dealing with the problems of Stifter's own time: one by Arno Schmidt (1958); the other by Horst Albert Glaser (1965).[32] The attack by Schmidt, as the sensational title *Der sanfte Unmensch* (The Gentle Brute) indicates, is arrogant, superficial, and crude, without betraying the slightest feeling for the beauty of the work. Glaser's criticism, written with more understanding, warrants discussion. The aim of his book, *Die Restauration des Schönen* (The Restoration of the Beautiful), is to combine sociologi-cal and esthetic viewpoints, to relate Stifter's utopia to the actual conditions of Austrian society, in conscious opposition to which Stifter wrote his novel.[33]

Glaser compares his method to that of the photographer. He wants to reverse the utopian negative to the positive of the cor-responding sociological reality. Uncovering the hidden sociological content of the novel, he says, will set off the utopia and, by way of contrast, show more clearly its specific qualities. This method of interpretation shows some of the weaknesses and limitations of the novel, but is too biased to do it justice and, more often than not, gives a distorted view. The cruel conclusion of Glaser's approach is that Stifter should have written *Der Nachsommer* in a way which would have made impossible the creation of this novel of "extended dream." Had Stifter included the real world of the *Vormärz,* the novel would have fallen apart, as Glaser himself admits.[34]

Glaser grants the novel only esthetic logic and truth, which become meaningless for him in the absence of historical reality or the possibility of future realization. Thus, he maintains, the utopia constantly turns its glance backward toward an agrarian, patriarchal feudalism, and Stifter considers the relations between rich and poor as natural and God-given. Most of the utopia, according to Glaser, has its origins in the miserable conditions, frustrations, and longings of the petty bourgeoisie to which Stifter belonged. This seems to me only partially true, as shown, for instance, by Stifter's relation to nature. His was not the sentimental longing of the politically and economically frustrated bourgeois, but a genuine intimacy with nature, which he acquired in his childhood and youth, and which never faded into pale memories while he lived in Vienna and Linz. Besides, had he not been, first and foremost, an artist, he might very well have been content with his position as a bourgeois

Schulrat in the provincial town of Linz, and the *Nachsommer* world would never have come into being. This world is not the *Pensionopolis,* for which the whining Schulrat yearned, as Glaser so deprecatingly says, or the world of *Rentiers,* as contemporary critics called it.[35] It is a consciously poetic creation, even though some of its origins are to be found in Stifter's personal life.

In his novel Stifter wanted to create an atmosphere which would lift the reader above ordinary life, where he would experience his own humanity more purely and completely.[36] Evidently this realm had to be restricted to an elite, not so much of birth as of natural disposition. Neither Risach nor Heinrich's father belongs to the nobility; both are self-made men of humble origin. To expect of the persons in the novel a Marxian consciousness, a guilt feeling about their wealth, whether acquired or inherited, is obviously absurd. Glaser wilfully overlooks the fact that Stifter could not attack any social ills of his time in the novel, since he objected to any kind of *littérature engagée.*[37] It is also a moot question how much he knew of those ills beyond the limited sphere of his official duties. There, as in the case of the grammar school teachers, he tried to remedy ills as best he could.

Within the novel, socioeconomic questions are not touched upon. Working hours and the pay of employees are not mentioned, but we can be sure that nobody is exploited. Human relationships are warm, unclouded by arrogance on the part of the rich and envy on the part of those in their service. Heinrich forms friendships with Eustach, with the gardener Simon and his wife, with the zither player Joseph, and with the mountain guide Kaspar. He makes sure to compensate people who work for him when he cannot finish the work for which he has hired them. Risach, recognizing Roland's artistic gift, allows him to develop it and finally gives him the money to go to Rome. He restores two Gothic altars out of his own pocket. Neither he nor Heinrich's father shuns his obligations to the community; Heinrich's father holds a public office without pay, Risach, through his example, teaches his neighbors better farming. Both enjoy the leisure of their Indian summer only after a long life of conscious dedication to their respective duties as statesman and merchant, although neither of them found full satisfaction in his profession. The closing sentences of the novel clearly state that Heinrich will continue his scientific pursuits. His life will be centered in his family, but he will, at the same time, try to become a useful member of society.

One might very well argue that all this is too vague, too private, and too incongruous with the actual conditions of the time. This argument is strengthened if one compares Stifter to a writer like Balzac, who so vividly portrayed the sinister aspects of rising capitalism, its ruthlessness and greed; or to Dickens, who did so much to draw attention to human misery in the wake of the Industrial Revolution. The utopian, timeless character of *Der Nachsommer,* the lack of political and sociological implications, the limited—mostly esthetic—activity of its protagonists does not diminish its greatness as a work of art, but narrows its place in world literature. This is one reason why Stifter will never reach the worldwide popularity of either Balzac or Dickens.

The reader of *Der Nachsommer* who has not read Glaser's book may easily overlook the absence of poverty or exploitation, but he will be aware of the absence of struggle, of "blood, sweat and tears," of evil, illness, death, and suffering, in the novel proper. That mental anguish is present, at least in the flashback, is as important in the artistic economy of the work as Heinrich's and Natalie's strong response to the performance of *King Lear.* Konrad Steffen, in his *Deutungen* (Interpretations), rightly stresses the polarity and balance between the novel proper and the flashback, in spite of their being so unequal in length. Without the flashback, he says, especially without the fervor of Mathilde's youth, the novel would not make sense. Heinrich and Natalie would be puppets.[38]

If, however, we judge the novel on philosophical grounds as an expression of Stifter's Weltanschauung, the absence of anything negative, of any harsh or bitter tone, the belief that all is best in this best of all possible worlds is harder to accept and is probably shared by very few modern readers. What are we to make, for instance, of such a naïve statement as that of Heinrich's father: "God directs the world in such a way that talents are properly distributed, so that every kind of work is done which has to be done on earth, and so that there will never be a time when all men are architects" (15). It seems to me that Stifter would have done much better not to attempt a rational justification of the ideal order of his *Nachsommer* world.

One cannot help feeling that Stifter subconsciously banned all suffering, all discord, all struggle from *Der Nachsommer* and some other late works, as if he could thus ban them out of existence. Quite in contrast to many of his earlier works, he does not reflect upon the mystery of fate, of human destiny, or of the indifference with which nature metes out bliss or disaster. He does not want to raise questions for which there are no answers. Faith in a benevolent God is taken for granted. No doubt ever ripples these undisturbed waters. It seems strange that in a work where so many aspects of human life are discussed, religion is not. Religious experience is limited to a feeling of awe vis-à-vis the beauty and grandeur of the universe, of gratitude toward this ever-benign God, and of quiet resignation to His will. Love of God is the highest, the only absolute form of love. Yet our human hearts cannot fully reach Him: we can only worship Him. But He gave us for our love on earth divers manifestations of the Divine. It is present in the love members of one family have for each other, in the love between bridegroom and bride, in the love between friends, in the love of fatherland, of art, of science, of nature. Even *Liebhabereien* (hobbies) are rivulets, branching from the mainstream of love. He whom the greater objects of love have left or who never had any, he who does not even have any *Liebhaberei,* scarcely lives, scarcely worships God, he just vegetates *(er ist nur da)* (634–35). Religious practices, such as going to church or making the sign of the cross, are rarely mentioned. One short sentence of a very general nature is allotted to Heinrich's and Natalie's wedding in the village church. It is easy to overlook or to forget that the protagonists of the novel are Catholics.

In a letter to Heckenast, where Stifter speaks of his aims in the novel, he equates religion with being truly human *(reine Menschlichkeit).*[39] When Heinrich's father promises that his son will do everything in his power to become a worthy member of his new family, he mentions first of all human dignity *(Menschenwürde)* without which nobody can be a part of the best human society (821). Stifter's expression *"bessere menschliche Gesellschaft"* is ambivalent, but it refers here not so much to social rank as to the best in human qualities. The predominantly humanistic attitude of *Der Nachsommer* puts the novel clearly in the tradition of German classicism. Stifter's *reine Menschlichkeit* echoes Goethe's beautiful verse, *"Alle mensch-*

liche Gebrechen/sühnet reine Menschlichkeit" (True humanity atones for all human failings).[40]

Der Nachsommer, more than any other work of Stifter, justifies his proud statement, "It is true, I am not Goethe, but one of his kin, and the seed of what is pure, noble, and simple also goes from my writings to the hearts of men" (*Br II,* 209). Thus Stifter wrote in 1854, while he was working on his novel. Shortly after its publication in 1857, he wrote to Heckenast that his work, created in sharp contrast to the moral depravity *(Verkommenheit)* of his time, would probably go unnoticed for a while but would triumph in the end. This had been the case with Goethe's greatest works, which made no impression at first (*Br III,* 93). And when, eight years later, he reread *Der Nachsommer,* he agreed with the impression of another reader, that it was a pity that Goethe could not have read it. He was more certain than in the case of any of his other works that the novel had a future, because of its being too deep for his own generation (*Br IV,* 273).

Stifter's prophecy proved right: *Der Nachsommer* did not come into its own until the twentieth century. It will, however, never become a popular novel. It will remain a great work of art for "The Happy Few" to whom Stendhal dedicated the second volume of his *History of Painting in Italy.* It is written for those who are willing to follow Stifter into a poetic realm of perfect beauty, to an island where *"tout n'est qu'ordre et beauté."*[41] It is written for those who still believe that the classic ideal of full and true humanity is a timeless one, which, in the last analysis, spells responsibility and not escapism. As Oskar Loerke puts it, "This old-fashioned world has never really existed, therefore it is not out-of-date. It is a higher life, a higher world."[42] The novel fully deserves a complete English translation, which is still lacking.

CHAPTER 6

Witiko

IF *Der Nachsommer* has met such a varied reception, this is equally, or even more, true of Stifter's second novel, *Witiko,* the third and last volume of which appeared in 1867, twenty years after its conception.[1] Lunding calls it "without doubt the strangest prose fiction in the 19th century," and Albrecht Schaeffer does not know of any work in European literature whose form has anything in common with *Witiko.*[2] It is, therefore, not surprising that evaluations of the novel range from wholesale condemnations to exaggerated panegyrics—it has even been called a sacred book! When it first appeared, only a few close friends and the Grand Duke Carl Alexander of Sachsen-Weimar, grandson of Goethe's patron and friend Karl August, were much impressed by the work. The Grand Duke bestowed the Order of the White Falcon on Stifter, together with a letter of appreciation. Stifter was especially pleased that Goethe was supposed to have contributed the motto "Be alert" (*Seid wachsam)* to the order. The contemporary reviews were overwhelmingly negative. Stifter was accused of having chosen subject matter of no interest to his time; of superabundance of detail; of lack of suspense, warmth, psychological insight; of using an archaic, wooden, artificial style. He was compared with Walter Scott—a comparison which necessarily told against him. He knew and liked Walter Scott, but *Witiko* was never intended to be an imitation of Scott's kind of novel. *Ivanhoe,* Scott's most popular novel, which, like *Witiko,* deals with twelfth-century history, illuminates the uniqueness of Stifter's narrative. *Witiko* possesses none of the elements which might, even today, thrill the readers of *Ivanhoe:* chivalric romance, magnanimous superheroes and heroines, cruel villains, and noble robbers. It lacks *Ivanhoe's* generally fast-moving, melodramatic action, its suspense, mysterious disguises, its horrors and last-minute rescues.

The negative attitude toward *Witiko* persisted for a long time. R. M. Meyer, a leading German literary historian at the turn of the century, saw in *Witiko* nothing but extreme mannerism, and this is how the novel strikes many a superficial reader today. Alfred Biese's much-used *Deutsche Literaturgeschichte* (1910) labeled it utterly unpalatable because of its prolixity. Even such a pioneer in Stifter research as Alois Raimund Hein could not appreciate *Witiko* as a whole.[3] It was Hermann Bahr in his *Adalbert Stifter: Eine Entdeckung* (1919) who first gave this novel undivided praise. But a decade later, Friedrich Gundolf called it a wretched *(unseliges)* book, which showed the decline of the aging writer, and which we had better forget if we want to honor Stifter's memory.[4] Hermann Hesse, on the other hand, giving Bahr full credit for his rediscovery of this completely forgotten work by Stifter, speaks of *Witiko* as a unique and movingly beautiful book. It is the only modern novel which gave him the feeling of an epic.[5] From Thomas Mann, we have a paradoxical statement about the special charm its monotony *(Langweiligkeit)* holds for him. He sees in *Witiko* one of the greatest and most encouraging vindications of *"Langeweile."*[6] He says that "the bold purity, daring pedantry, spiritual uniqueness of this masterpiece" brought him "much solace and joy" at the beginning of his odyssey after Hitler came to power.[7] The German theologian Bonhoeffer, awaiting trial in a Nazi prison, had a similar experience: "My overriding experience for the last ten days has been *Witiko*. . . . For me it is one of the finest books I know. The purity of its style and character drawing gives one a quite rare and peculiar feeling of happiness."[8] No other praise could have given Stifter greater satisfaction. Except for *Witiko,* I know only of some verse by Goethe to which such moving testimony was given by victims of Nazi persecution.[9]

Witiko is a difficult book because of its peculiar style and the remoteness of its subject. Witiko, the hero, is the last descendant of a once-powerful noble family, which traces its origin to the Roman Ursini.[10] No longer powerful or rich, the family possesses only a few small pieces of land. One of these is located in the valley of Plana or Plan, that is, Stifter's birthplace. The novel begins in the year 1138 with young Witiko riding from Passau to Bohemia in order to seek his fortune. This we learn from a conversation with Bertha, a young girl whom he encounters at a clearing in the woods. She is wearing a crown of wild roses, and Witiko takes this as a good omen, because wild roses have always had great significance for his family. The rose symbol accompanies us throughout the novel, signifying good luck and achievement, faithful love and happiness. Witiko is no ordinary adventurer; he is in quest of a great fortune befitting a true man. The German *"dem rechten Manne"* has the implications of true, right, brave, and good. The words *"recht," "das Rechte," "das Recht," "gerecht"* (just), *"Gerechtigkeit"* (justice) are the key words of the novel. Witiko's tenaciousness, patience, good fortune—and Stifter's optimism—enable him to acquire a fief, riches, a wife from a leading family, without ever violating the dictates of his conscience. His life story is closely interwoven with the history of Bohemia during the critical years between 1138 and 1158, and to a lesser extent also with that of the Holy Roman Empire.

In 1140, Duke Soběslaw is dying, and the question arises who shall succeed him—his son Wladislaw or his nephew by the same name. His son is only twenty-one years of age, but the nobles of Bohemia and Moravia had acknowledged him as their future ruler at the assembly of Sadska, held two years earlier. His nephew is a little older and seems the better man for the difficult task. Soběslaw sends Witiko to Prague, where the nobles have assembled at the ancient castle of Wišehrad, to reconsider the election of the future duke. Witiko, young and unknown, risks his life in trying to be admitted as a listener to the illustrious assembly. After a violent debate, he is granted permission to stay. Long deliberations follow, delving deeply into the previous history of Bohemia. Finally the choice falls on the nephew. Some older men have raised their voice for the son, because they consider it morally wrong (*unrecht*) to forgo the allegiance given to him earlier at Sadska. The most outspoken among them is Silvester, the Bishop of Prague.

After his defeat in the assembly, Silvester resigns from his high office; we shall meet him later as a humble monk tending his vegetables. Witiko hastens back to Soběslaw to bring him the sad news. Shortly before his death, however, Soběslaw advises his son to surrender to his cousin and utters the prophetic, but at this point still mysterious, words "Načerat will not win the victory over Wladislaw" (V, 158). After Soběslaw's death, the new Duke sends for Witiko, whom he had met by chance when Witiko first set out on his quest. He wants Witiko to serve him, but Witiko wants to wait, in order to "collect his thoughts."

What follows can be summed up as a series of rebellions against the new Duke. Načerat is the leader of the opposition. The nobles are dissatisfied with the Duke, because he is just and has the welfare of the people in mind, instead of satisfying their egoistic desires for power and wealth. They put up a Counter-Duke—Konrad of Znaim, Duke of Moravia. After young Wladislaw, Sobéslaw's son, has surrendered to Konrad his right to the throne, Witiko feels free of any moral obligation toward him. Witiko becomes a staunch supporter of Duke Wladislaw and, together with men from his woodlands, whose leader he becomes, helps the Duke more than once to put down the rebellions. The highlights of this long struggle are the battle at the Mountain Wysoka, the unsuccessful siege of Prague by the enemy, and the final victory over Konrad of Znaim.

Duke Wladislaw turns out to be not only the legitimate *(rechtmäs-sige)* duke, but also the right *(rechte)* person to rule: he is just, forgiving, moderate, humane, and grateful.[11] He and Witiko become friends and allies in the greater fellowship of men of good will *(Bund der Guten)*. After victory is won, Witiko is most generously rewarded and can build his castle, the Witikohaus.[12] He can marry Bertha, many years after their first meeting. Twice again he has to leave for war. With Duke Wladislaw, he comes to the aid of the Emperor Frederick Barbarossa in his fight against the rebellious Italian cities, especially Milan. At the very end of the novel, he attends the famous Reichstag held by Frederick Barbarossa in Mainz at Whitsuntide 1184.

Political and military actions alternate with domestic scenes, where Witiko, especially during his first stay in the valley of Plana, takes an active part in the life of the community and shares its frugal way of life. Among other things, this novel is a nostalgic return to the scenes of Stifter's childhood and youth, a hymn to his native woods, to the strength, simplicity, loyalty, and goodness of their inhabitants. The agility, toughness, and endurance acquired through their hard life in the forest enable these men to turn the tide in every battle under the leadership of Witiko. Because of their difficult life they are very practical people. They take along big sacks in which to put their booty, and they look upon war as a perfectly legitimate means of adding to their meager livelihood. One of the minor nobles of the woods says, "I went to war in order that right should prevail, that the oppressor be punished, and that a small landowner might perhaps expand a little" (334).

All the wars in which Witiko and his men participate are "just" wars. This is hammered into the reader's mind at every opportunity. History, for Stifter, is nothing but a final triumph of the moral law: the good will be rewarded; the bad, punished.[13] Whether the moral balance was in reality as neat as Stifter wants us to believe in *Witiko* is highly questionable. In his article, "Stifter's 'Witiko' und die geschichtliche Welt," Hermann Blumenthal shows in a few concrete examples how Stifter occasionally retouched history by suppressing egotistic or strictly political motives in his heroes. Blumenthal also points out that, for Stifter, the cities of northern Italy which resisted the Holy Roman Empire of Barbarossa were nothing but breakers of the law, whereas for his source, Raumer, they had a political right of their own.[14] Lunding remarks that, although Stifter could not come to terms with the "sneering amorality of history," he was determined to maintain the appearance of serene optimism and to awaken belief in an ordered universe, ruled by his gentle law. Rychner speaks of the optimism that Stifter as a moralist deliberately read into history.[15]

The philosophical issue of the morality of history must necessarily become clouded in a novel about the Middle Ages, where the religious and the secular are completely fused. "Justice must triumph, because it is valid in heaven and on earth," is the leitmotif of Dimut, a "Bohemian Joan of Arc" (254, 330, 625). Battle cries include in one breath "God, the Holy Trinity, the Empire and the King" (393). Before the Italian campaign, relics are placed in a church "for the glory of God and the sake of the enterprise" (929). The naïve woodlanders, Witiko's men, think nothing of offering a part of their booty to the Church (985). God and the saints are always on the side of right and justice; the Duke and his warriors never forget to pray to them before battle and to thank them after victory. Only once in the novel is there a hint that the other side might make the same claim. The very old Bolemil, who has seen many civil wars in his lifetime, says that the national saint, Saint Wenceslaus, may be of no avail to them in this present war, since both sides can ask for his help (349).

A war of defense, a war for right and justice is a "holy" war, and those slain in it will find their reward in heaven. This is in keeping with the spirit of the Middle Ages, but modern man is wary of "just" and "holy" wars and rewards in heaven, all the more as this way of thinking is by no means a thing of the past.[16] Modern man shudders to read of war sent by God as a means of purification and atonement for wrongdoing, even though we do not have to identify the speaker, the Bishop of Prague, with Stifter (639).[17] We feel uneasy about a father who would rather see his three very young sons die than suffer the arrogance of the enemy (269), or about a husband who wants to console his wife with the fact that their son died a "heroic" death (310). The pacifist Stifter is hard put to deal with a century where personal feuds, wars of succession, and rebellions were the order of the day. Stifter takes infinite pains to prove that the "good" ruler resorts to war only after all negotiations have failed. In order to justify war to his woodmen, Witiko speaks of the enemy as being worse than wolves, since the enemy acts from greed and not from hunger (696). This is a far cry from the earlier war story *Bergmilch*. There only the chauvinistic lord of the castle compares the enemies to wolves which one has to kill, whereas his wife still sees the human beings in them (III, 327-28). The constant need which Stifter feels to justify fighting in *Witiko* seems like an anachronism in the twelfth century. Even more of an anachronism is Duke Wladislaw's enlightened vision of a time when nations will act like individual beings, helping each other like friends and neighbors (353). Later on in the novel, he even wishes for a federation of all European nations (917).

Actual fighting, although vividly and convincingly depicted, occupies only about a twentieth part of the novel. Much more space is given to the description of councils, negotiations, preparations for battles and their aftermaths. War on Wladislaw's side is conducted in a more humane fashion than it was in the Middle Ages, or, for that matter, at any time. The idea of humane warfare is one of the greatest human fallacies. The burning pitch thrown from the battlements of Prague foreshadows napalm. Senseless devastation is strictly, but vainly, forbidden by Wladislaw: "And thus the warriors descended like a cloud on the land" (702). All the Duke can do is punish the perpetrators of the crime afterward (706). After battles, a list of the dead is compiled (if possible) before they are buried, and great, loving care is given to the wounded. Once, even an emergency hospital is erected, and a physician from the Duke's camp is sent to the wounded (697)! When, at the end of a campaign, rewards are distributed, the wounded receive special consideration (439). The families of the dead are compensated, and Witiko comforts the mothers (443).

Men are wounded or die in battle, villages are burned, cattle are taken away, crops are destroyed, but nowhere are suffering and deprivation described in naturalistic detail. It is very easy to overlook the torture of Bishop Zdik's men (879) or the order to cut off the hands of those who tried to smuggle food into beleaguered Milan (982), because Stifter mentions both facts so casually. The very young fighters, Urban's nephew and Osel's three sons, are spared serious injury or death. Wounds heal, and Tom the Fiddler, whose right hand was injured, is capable of playing at Witiko's wedding, by means of an ingenious, although highly improbable, device. Had Stifter ever experienced the horrors of war himself, he could not have maintained this optimistic outlook.[18] The strongest pacifist plea in the novel is Witiko's laconic reply to the troubadour von Kürenberg's praise of war as glorious. "To us," Witiko says, "it brought destruction and sorrow" (568).

In contrast to Stifter's other works, *Witiko,* because of its very subject matter, contains a good deal of hero worship and praise of bodily strength and courage, manliness, honor, and fame. Only once does Stifter's skepticism toward this customary way of thinking find its expression in *Witiko*—in the remarkable figure of Agnes, the daughter of the German Emperor Henry IV. When Witiko speaks to her of knightly deeds he wants to accomplish in order to win glory and fame for himself, Agnes answers, "This young knight again speaks of deeds . . . do we know, after all, what deeds are?" (532). A little later, after giving a moving account of her own life and the woeful end of her father, she says:

I have seen enough deeds which have been praised and have caused evil. He who loves his wife, educates his children in the love of God. increases his possessions honestly, protects and improves the life of his subjects, has performed the right kind of deeds. And who knows whether it is not a better pursuit to embroider this piece of cloth to serve the Church or to soften the footsteps of an old man than to conquer and destroy duchies. (541–42)

Agnes's words are more in accord with Stifter's general views on what is truly great, than a cliché like Bertha's parting words to Witiko before he goes to war: "Witiko, you are a man. Be a man, and think of those at home" (927). Although on the "just"—that is, Duke Wladislaw's—side, the war is conducted as humanely as possible, there is still more violence to be found in *Witiko* than in any other work of Stifter. Abuse is heaped on the enemy, and vulgar words, found nowhere else in Stifter's work, are employed. Violent emotions—anger, desire for revenge, fury in the heat of battle—are depicted. There is nothing "gentle" in the battle scenes; to see, with Steffen, the gentle law still at work in the death-dealing weapon of the smith of Plan, is to deprive the word "gentle" of its meaning. Neither Steffen nor, for that matter, Stifter himself, wants to face the deep conflict which man encounters when he tries to punish violations of the gentle law, and then no longer can act in accordance with the law itself that demands "that every human being be protected as a jewel, inasmuch as every man is a jewel for all other men" (III, 11).[19]

Witiko has been hailed by several modern critics as a model for political conduct. They base their claim on the high humanity, the sense of right and justice which animate the political leaders in the novel. We do not for one moment want to deny that such high ethics should prevail in politics. But it is hard for modern man to make the necessary analogies between the Middle Ages and our own time. In *Witiko,* we do not deal with a "timeless humanity," as Hüller wants us to believe. Witiko is a Christian knight and not a "classical antique figure" *(Gestalt).*[20] Life and politics in *Witiko* are God- and Church-centered; in our times they are not. The ideas of a Holy Empire and a divinely appointed ruler, which play such an important part toward the end of the novel, are alien to us, or idolatrous, if they appear in secular form, as in Hitler's case.

Our social structure also differs in every respect from that of the twelfth century. At that time, man's station in life was thought to be ordered by God; for the true Christian any rebellion against authority was sin (333, 389, 392, 800). Man's first allegiance was to God; his second, almost equally strong allegiance, to his lord. Feudal society was held together by highly personal, mutual bonds of loyalty, trust, and gratitude. Witiko's relationship to Soběslaw and Wladislaw as their vassal, his relationship to his woodlanders as their leader and then their lord, are examples of such bonds. But such personal relationships, though beautiful and admirable, unfortunately, no longer suffice in modern mass society. We tend to forget that toward the end of the novel, Witiko becomes a feudal lord like his ancestors, because he is such an ideal feudal lord in his kindness, justice, and concern for his subjects, who love him and look upon him as one of themselves. But their claim that they chose him as their lord *("Heil*

dem guten Witiko, den wir zu unserem Herrn erkoren haben"
[741]*),* is invalid, for it was the Duke who gave Witiko the land.
Witiko generously absolves his new subjects of one-tenth of the
tribute they formerly owed the Duke; this means, of course, that
nine-tenths remain. Witiko wants to remain humble, but the
chivalric code of honor sets him apart from, and above, his men
(832–33). It is easy to understand that criticism in Stifter's own time
found glorification of feudalism inappropriate at a moment when
attempts were being made to get rid of the last vestiges of feudalism.[21]

One might, however, try to abstract a generally valid core of political wisdom from this medieval novel and take as ethical guidelines
for political conduct the often quoted dialogue between Witiko and
Cardinal Guido, the papal legate. After being praised by the Cardinal,
Witiko modestly replies, "I tried to do what the nature of things
requires. . . ." Whereupon the Cardinal answers," If you strive to do
what the nature of things requires, it would be good if all men knew
what the nature of things requires and acted in accordance with it,
because then they would fulfill the will of God." But Witiko is still
not satisfied and says, "Often I do not know what the nature of things
requires." The Cardinal concludes the discussion with the laconic
remark, *"Dann folge dem Gewissen, und du folgst den Dingen"*
(Then follow your conscience and you will fulfill what the nature of
things demands) (816).[22] These words sound at first like a magic
formula, an infallible guide in the most difficult situations. But our
conscience can guide us only after we have a clear insight into the
nature of things, into a given situation, and Witiko had just acknowledged that he is often lacking this insight.

In his book on *Witiko,* Weippert sees the problem, but tries to
resolve it by making a rather unconvincing distinction between
complete, scientific knowledge of the nature of things and that which
is needed for action at a given moment without violating the nature
of things.[23] Two incidents in the novel itself show that the question
is more complicated than the hypnotic words, *"Folge dem Gewissen,
und du folgst den Dingen,"* would indicate. The first occurs at the
assembly on the Wišehrad. To Bishop Silvester it is absolutely clear
that conscience requires keeping one's oath and letting Sobĕslaw's
son ascend the throne, even though the nephew is the better man.
God, he argues, can save the country through the boy Wladislaw.
Bishop Zdik, a thoroughly honest and unselfish man, acts in good

conscience when he advises the assembly to elect the nephew—as do many good men along with him. There is no comment by Stifter, and the reader must draw his own conclusions. Are we to believe that Zdik did not probe his conscience deeply enough? His later repentance favors such an interpretation. But in the reader's mind the question remains, what would have happened if the absolute dictates of conscience had been followed and young Wladislaw, who turns out to be an extremely weak character, had ascended the throne. Would he have been able to prevent civil war? Would he not have been a helpless tool in the hands of such selfish men as Načerat and his followers?

The other case where Silvester represents an ethical standard differing from that of the actively engaged person is the much-discussed incident at Holobkau near Pilsen. In a chance encounter, Witiko lets three of the rebellious princes escape so that they can tell Konrad of Znaim of the superior strength of the Duke's army and the hopelessness of their fighting him. Witiko wants to prevent further bloodshed and also—this we learn much later—to keep the Duke from having to punish the rebellious princes immediately and thus perhaps too harshly (678). Witiko is not sure, however, whether acting on his own could be called "good" in the opinion of the highest ethical arbiter he knows—Bishop Silvester. When he asks him, the answer, somewhat to our surprise, is negative. Witiko, the Bishop says, had overstepped his duty as a soldier (450). Yet he, as well as Bishop Zdik, had acted in good faith *("nach meinem guten Sinne")*.

The mild, almost mock, punishment which Witiko receives at the hands of the Duke for his arbitrary action as a soldier is a good example of how Stifter avoided the tragic in his later work. How differently the same conflict is treated by Kleist in his drama *Prinz Friedrich von Homburg*! Silvester is the purest incarnation of the ethical ideal in the novel; the others can only approximate it. He is, on another level, the spiritual brother of the priest in *Kalkstein*, equally humble and lovable. Does Stifter mean to intimate, as Lunding suggests, that only the man of God, renouncing all earthly goods and his high office, withdrawing to the solitude of the monastery, is able to express the ethical ideal consistently, whereas the worldly knight Witiko cannot withdraw into solitude, but after a period of deliberation must take the risk of choice?[24] The conflict between an absolute ethical ideal and any involvement in action, a conflict, at which Stifter only hints in *Witiko,* brings to mind Goethe's profound remark: *"Der Handelnde ist immer gewissenlos; es hat niemand Gewissen als der Betrachtende"* (The man of action is always without conscience, it is only the observer who has a conscience).[25]

Even if we assume that the modern reader finds interest in a subject so remote from him as the internecine wars of twelfth century Bohemia, there still remains the hurdle of a highly stylized form with its lack of individualization and psychological depth. Stifter wanted to write a novel showing the triumph of moral law, not so much in the fate of individuals, as in that of entire nations. As he wrote to Heckenast on June 8, 1861, he wanted to write a novel with history as its main subject and individual characters as a matter of secondary importance. They are carried, he said, by the broad current of history which, at the same time, they help to form. The so-called historical novel is, for him, an "epic in prose." Thus he unfolds before us an immense canvas of people, shown at times in violent action, but more often in slow motion. He purposely avoids any psychological probing and any personal comment. Objectivity is his goal, and what cannot be shown outwardly is not shown at all.

Witiko is even less of an individual than Heinrich Drendorf in *Der Nachsommer.* He shows no real growth; there is no Risach, no *Rosenhaus* to open up new horizons for him. He has to observe the political developments in order to take sides. But, from the very beginning, he is reserved, prudent, self-controlled, loyal, and grateful. Wherever he goes, he takes care of his horse himself. Stifter never forgets to mention this trait as a symbol of Witiko's equal concern for matters small or big. How "good" he is we learn from testimonies by people close to him—a device Stifter often uses in his works. Witiko shares Heinrich's deadly seriousness, his complete lack of any sense of humor. He never displays any characteristics of youth, such as abandon, exuberance or imprudence. He rarely shows any emotion. He weeps over Soběslaw's death and has tears in his eyes when he sees his mother after an absence of four years. But he later tells his future father-in-law that he stayed with her as long as propriety *(die Gebühr)* demanded (757). He remains cool even in the heat of battle, as the Holobkau episode demonstrates. We may admire him, but we feel no true empathy with this knight "without fear and without reproach." Witiko's leather clothes, which he wears most of the time in "joy and sorrow" (570), are symbols of the value he attaches to reliability rather than brilliant appearance. The Scarlet Rider and other splendidly clad knights good-naturedly nickname him "Leatherman."

The other characters have even less individuality than Witiko; they are prototypes. Wladislaw is the ideal ruler, *"ein schattenlos edler Schöner"* (a beautiful noble figure without blemish),[26] Odolen a daredevil youth, Bolemil a wise old man, Načerat a demagogue and archtraitor, Silvester a man of almost Christlike kindness and simplicity. To the great number of individuals who take part in the action is added an even greater number of persons of whom we learn only the names and sometimes the offices. There is frequently a long listing of names in order to produce the impression of large crowds. But used too often, this device becomes fatiguing. Many of these persons we meet more than once, and we cannot help marveling that Stifter never loses sight of them, even after long intervals. Yet, we get somehow lost in this maze of names—at least when we read the novel for the first time. Max Stefl even found it necessary to add an index of persons to his Insel edition.

In order to appreciate *Witiko,* one has to study its structure as one would study a musical composition or an intricately woven tapestry. There is a rhythmic, orderly pattern in *Witiko,* as there is in nature with its constant change of seasons. War and peace, destroying and building, alternate in the novel. The same people reappear at well-spaced intervals. Certain patterns of action and behavior are repeated throughout. Perhaps the most typical example is the conduct of war with its identical sequence of events: the preparations for the campaign, the blessing of the departing warriors, the council, the futile, last-minute negotiations with the enemy, the prayer before battle, the actual fighting, the prayer of thanks after victory, the expression of gratitude and the distribution of rewards by the leaders. Other frequently used patterns are the paying and returning of visits, and the giving or exchanging of gifts. There are, of course, nuances, according to the wealth of host or giver. A sign of Witiko's having "arrived," for example, is the elaborate ritual with which he welcomes into his home Boreš, the castellan of the late Soběslaw, to whom Duke Wladislaw and his wife have entrusted their wedding gifts for Witiko and Bertha (856). The presentation of these exquisite gifts necessitates an even more elaborate ritual (858–66).

The basic principle of a highly stylized form, repetition, shows up strikingly in the spoken word. The readers of *Witiko* are startled or appalled, as the case may be, by its excessive use in the novel. Repetition of the same words or sentences is warranted, as Lunding has pointed out, when legal questions arise in council, and is thus quite frequently and effectively used by Stifter. Repetition is also appropriate on other solemn occasions, for example, when Witiko asks for Bertha's hand in marriage or at the above-mentioned presentation of wedding gifts. (The strictly regulated code of chivalric behavior met halfway Stifter's own tendency toward ceremonious speech.) Repetition, however, is unrealistic in the dialogue between Witiko and Bertha when, after six years, they revisit the clearing in the woods where they had first met. One lover picks up the words of the other six times in succession (767). At such a moment of strong emotion we expect a more artless expression, maybe even silence. Yet it should be emphasized that the terms "realistic" or "unrealistic" are not used to determine the esthetic value of the novel. This "strange" dialogue has a charm of its own and is entirely in keeping with the style of the work.

In order to be just to Stifter, one has to acknowledge, as Lunding has noted, that he also masters other, less stylized, and less abstract, modes of expression. There are, for instance, the dramatic battle scenes, the elaborate, greatly varied speeches in the elective assembly on the Wyšehrad, and Načerat's clever speech at the unofficial meeting of the Bohemian and Moravian nobles, a model of demagoguery, which strongly reminds us of Mark Antony's famous funeral oration in Shakespeare's *Julius Caesar.*

A detailed analysis of *Witiko's* style is beyond the scope of this study. The main characteristics other than repetition are the prodigious epic breadth (where everything—great or small—is of equal significance), the simple syntax with its preference for coordination, the extreme scarcity of embellishing adjectives, of images and metaphors, the rare show of emotion, and the complete absence of any comment by the author. This factual style, which often verges on the dry, affects readers in different ways. Some will find it boring, whereas others will find that it conveys great peace and quiet. Most readers, however, will agree that this sober, restrained style reaches great heights in some passages, among the finest Stifter has written, the most moving being perhaps the short description of Soběslaw's death (158–59).

One aspect of the style which, to my knowledge, has been neglected by the critics, is the wide use of color for design and vivid visual impressions. Thus, the color of banners differentiates various groups in battles. The speakers in the elective assembly on the Wyšeh-rad are first identified only by what Witiko sees—the color of their hair, their beards, their eyes, their tunics, their caps and the feathers on them—before they identify themselves by name. This principle of identifying a person by his clothing is used throughout the novel. Stifter's desire to present only what can be seen immediately merges with the painter's delight in the colorful clothing of the Middle Ages. He always carefully harmonizes the color of hair, beard, and eyes with that of the clothing, as well as the colors of horses and riders. If there are crowds, brilliant *tableaux vivants* appear. It would be an interesting experiment to try to reproduce some of these with the brush.

Colors are used as leitmotifs and symbols. As with Risach, the greater the man, the simpler the clothing. Weak, young Wladislaw (Soběslaw's son) and the traitor Načerat wear splendid clothes in rich colors. Wladislaw is compared to a blue butterfly glittering in the sun (269). The Duke, on the other hand, after he has ascended the throne, wears a simple brown tunic, and his wife chooses the same color. As a carefree youth the Duke wore bright scarlet, and Stifter called him the Scarlet Rider. Very effective color contrasts are used to show the transitoriness of all earthly glory. Red blood soils the coat of horses and the shining clothes of men dying in battle. Their rosy faces turn ash-gray (303–4). No further comment by the author is needed.

All that has been said in this short analysis of *Witiko* is intended to show, among other things, that only patient rereading will open up the work to the reader. If I were to speculate on future critical evaluations of *Witiko*, I should be inclined to agree with Lunding that categorical value judgments are out of place and that the evaluation will fluctuate with the tastes of individuals and epochs.[27] The number of people able to enjoy *Witiko* will be even smaller than in the case of *Der Nachsommer.* Like *Der Nachsommer,* the work has not yet found an English translator.

CHAPTER 7

Late Tales and the Last Version of
Die Mappe meines Urgrossvaters

O F the stories which Stifter wrote while he was working on
Witiko, only two seem to deserve close analysis:
Nachkommenschaften (Chips off the Old Block, 1864), and
Der Waldbrunnen (The Fountain in the Woods, 1866). *Nachkommenschaften* is the story of the Roderer family, whose motto
could be called "all or nothing." This single-mindedness is also
typical of other Stifterian characters, such as Hugo in *Das alte
Siegel,* Tiburius in *Der Waldsteig,* Erwin in *Die drei Schmiede
ihres Schicksals.* With complete absorption, the Roderers pursue
one goal, only to abandon it in the end and conclude their lives in
an entirely different fashion.

Nachkommenschaften centers in a young artist, Friedrich Roderer,
and an older man, Peter Roderer, who turn out to be distantly
related. In his youth Peter Roderer had vainly tried to surpass all
epic poets and capture "absolute truth" *(wirkliche Wahrheit)* in
his epic poems. He had destroyed them all and, after the death of
his father, had spent the same concentrated energy on becoming a
successful businessman. The knowledge of foreign languages which
he had acquired in order to read many epic poems was of great help
to him. At the beginning of the story, we find him a model gentleman-
farmer, having chosen for his *"Nachsommer"* agriculture, "the
oldest occupation of mankind" (603). The relationship between
the two Roderers is one already familiar to us from Stifter's earlier
works: a young man learning through his association with an older
man. The scene is one of Stifter's favorite, unassuming, rather
melancholy landscapes—a moor with some adjoining pine woods
and the inevitable blue mountains in the distance. The older man
wants to drain the moor, while the younger wants to put it on
canvas in all its "somber simplicity and grandeur" (635). Being a
Roderer, however, he does not succeed; in the end he marries Peter

Roderer's beautiful daughter Susanna and destroys the painting on which he had worked so long and arduously.

The young painter is a slightly ironical self-portrait of the young Stifter who, as we know from his letters, often relentlessly reworked his paintings and then destroyed them.[1] There are other autobiographical details in the older Roderer's life: the father's linen and flax trade, his love of reading, and the account of his untimely death. The words which Peter Roderer's mother uses to express a mother's infinite joy in her children are taken verbatim from one of Stifter's letters.[2]

While Stifter, in his usual fashion, was making countless changes in the manuscript, he wrote to Amalia on October 20, 1863, "Maybe I am myself a Roderer after all." But whereas in this letter, as in many others, we feel the agony of the artist who is never completely satisfied with his work, in the story the same topic is treated with a light, humorous touch. Nowhere in his work has Stifter given us a true portrait of the artist. When he comes close to it, as in *Zwei Schwestern,* he avoids tragedy by means of a highly improbable twist. Friedrich Roderer could very well have become a tragic figure like the painter Frenhofer in Balzac's *Le Chef-d'œuvre inconnu.* Competing with nature, he has tried for ten years to create the perfect painting of a nude. He literally loses his mind in the strife. When he finally shows two artists his "masterpiece," nothing is to be seen but part of a beautifully painted foot and a chaos of lines and colors. Only in a humorous story can we believe that a man so obsessed with painting as Friedrich Roderer, a man who finds such immense joy in this activity, will give it up so easily and painlessly, never to touch a brush again. Blackall suggests that Friedrich is not a true artist, but a dilettante, because of his false conception of art.[3] If Stifter intended Friedrich's conception of art to be false, however, why does he have Friedrich express his esthetic theory in the same words as Heinrich in *Der Nachsommer,* or as he himself does in the little essay "Über Kunst"?

The artist has to strive for "wirkliche Wirklichkeit" (reality itself), Friedrich argues, since he cannot surpass God, whose creation is his subject. God's world is "real" and, at the same time, full of poetry and unlimited power to move us. The task of the true artist is to portray nature faithfully, catching simultaneously the divine element it contains. To prove his point, Friedrich mentions a landscape by Ruysdael which, in spite of its extreme simplicity, affects the spectator forcefully.[4] Stifter does subscribe to Friedrich's concept of art. It is not his being a dilettante but his being a Roderer which makes him give up his art.

In the family history of the Roderers, Stifter shows his interest in the question of heredity, as he had done much earlier in *Die Narrenburg*. The Roderers exhibit all kinds of human folly and instability. But Peter Roderer, Susanna's father, hopes that his branch of the family will overcome these traits, settle on the moor, complete its drainage, grow calm and stable, help its neighbors and become one with them. In all likelihood, Friedrich and Susanna will fulfill the old man's dream and thus take the curse from at least a part of the Roderer family, as Heinrich and Anna do for the whole Scharnast family in *Die Narrenburg*.

Der Waldbrunnen is more serious than *Nachkommenschaften*. It is the story of an old man, Stephan Heilkun, who spends his summers in the country, together with his two grandchildren, Franz and Katharina. There he wants to regain, through the therapeutic powers of pure air and water, the "gaiety and health" of which the disappointments of his life have robbed him. These are very similar to Stifter's own disappointments in marriage and office and in the loss of the people dearest to him. The story takes place in the region of the *Lakerhäuser,* at the foot of the *Dreisesselberg,* where Stifter himself sought recreation. What Heilkun gains is something perhaps even more valuable than "gaiety and health"— the confidence and love of a shy child of nature. It is significant that Stifter gives the girl the name of his late foster daughter Juliana. The old man wins the girl's love through understanding and patience, qualities sorely lacking in her village teacher. Heilkun is careful not to give any valuable presents to the child or her half-crazed grandmother, on whom she has lavished all her love before she met him. During his second stay at the little house in the country, Heilkun realizes that he has received the most precious human gift, that is, being loved for one's own sake, rather than through blood bonds, out of gratitude or in expectation of future gifts (III, 673). The story is profoundly moving because Stifter, without becoming sentimental, makes us once more aware of man's basic loneliness. At the beginning, we see an old man who still feels "a lack of love," although, as his innocent grandson tells him, all the people around him "love" him, including himself and his sister. Stifter intimates how loosely we often use the word love. Heilkun's old age recalls the loneliness of Georg in *Der Waldgänger,* of Jodok in *Die Narrenburg,* of Hugo in *Das alte Siegel,* of the uncle in *Der Hagestolz.* These men, it is true, are more or less responsible for the loneliness of their old age, but the unutterable sadness of their condition haunts the reader all the same.

Just as impressive as the aura of loneliness surrounding Heilkun is the imaginative power with which Stifter evokes the picture of the beautiful, strange, shy, and passionate girl. Dialogue is sparse; spontaneous gestures often replace words. Juliana never uses the word "love" in referring to her grandmother; instead, she adorns her with everything colorful she finds or which Heilkun gives her, never keeping anything for herself. Bedecked with flowers, ribbons and feathers, the old woman presents a weird spectacle, which the unobservant village teacher misinterprets as mockery on the part of the girl. Her growing love for Heilkun is shown in a last-minute embrace when he leaves or her waiting for his return in the spring, in shy, caressing gestures, in her giving the little presents she gathers in the woods to him instead of to the children. Her strange, poetic ways are revealed through the odd words she writes into her copybook at school, which she shows only to Heilkun. Her poetic gift, as well as her extraordinary beauty, is also shown when she stands on the stone near the fountain, raising her slender body and her arms, uttering some bizarre rhymes referring to her grandmother (663–64). At another time, we watch her on the stone reciting, in her deep sonorous voice, some verses she had learned from Franz, Heilkun's grandson. The choice of verses and the way Stifter has the girl alter them are highly ingenious. She recites only fragments, sometimes repeating the same words over and over again. Most of the verses are by Goethe, and highly emotional ones at that. The first one reads:

> *Heiss mich nicht reden, heiss mich schweigen,*
> *Denn mein Geheimnis ist eine Pflicht;*
> *Ich möchte Dir mein ganzes Innre zeigen,*
> *Allein das Schicksal will es nicht!*

It is the first stanza of a poem Mignon recites in *Wilhelm Meisters Lehrjahre.*[5] Thus a subtle link between Juliana and Mignon is established. Franz and Juliana fall in love. Heilkun wants to take

Juliana home with him in the autumn in order to have her educated, so that in time she may become a suitable bride for Franz. But Juliana does not want to leave her grandmother, for whom, as she says, she is at once "mother, sister, governor, maid" (676). Heilkun then tells the girl that he cannot return and that Franz must forget her. After two summers, however, he does return. We guess that Franz, in spite of being away from Juliana, was not able to forget her. In time the grandmother dies. Juliana's mother and aunt weep at the funeral and tell everybody how good the old woman had been. Juliana is silent. Not unlike Cordelia's love for her father in *King Lear,* Juliana's had expressed itself in deeds, not words. She is now free to leave with Heilkun and his grandchildren. A few years later, she marries Franz. Nothing is said about this interval and the change which must have occurred in Juliana. It seems debatable whether this highly original child of nature, perhaps of gypsy origin, would ever have completely fitted into the usual pattern of society. The tragic ending of *Katzensilber,* where the dark-skinned girl disappears into the woods whence she had come, never to be seen again, seems more poetic and true. We have to admit, however, that Juliana is less wild and mysterious than the girl in *Katzensilber.* Stifter needed a happy ending to fulfill his dream for his foster daughter Juliana, who was also in many ways a strange girl. She had never found happiness and, while still very young, had committed suicide. In addition to this personal motif, Stifter may simply have shunned a tragic ending. None of his late works ends tragically.

The composition of *Der Waldbrunnen* is rather intricate. As so often with Stifter, it is a story within a story. The narrator, in whom we can partly recognize Stifter himself, begins by describing the two most beautiful human beings he has ever seen, more beautiful than Raphael's Sistine Madonna or any of the Greek statues he admired so much. One was a gypsy girl he had encountered on a trip as *Schulrat,* the other a young married woman he had seen on the Rigi mountain, which he had climbed with some fellow students. Both had perfectly proportioned bodies, a skin the color of old bronze, black hair and black eyes. He tells his wife about them, forestalling any possible jealousy by making it quite clear that the pleasure they had given him was completely disinterested. Then follows the story proper, which somebody had told him. The narrative closes with a short paragraph recounting a second visit to the Rigi, this time undertaken with his wife.[6] The innkeeper tells the narrator that the beautiful young woman in whom he had taken such an interest on his first visit, had been there again, accompanied by her husband and her sister-in-law and the latter's husband. He looks up the guestbook and finds the names Franz von Heilkun and Juliana von Heilkun for both visits. He now knows that the stunningly beautiful, well-dressed woman of his first visit on the Rigi had been no other than the shy, wild girl of the story.

The composition within the story is also remarkable. Heilkun's numerous visits to the country are tied together by the recurring change of seasons and various leitmotifs—very much as in *Katzensilber*. The little field, surrounded by bushes, belonging to Juliana's family, planted successively with rye, oats, barley, and rye again, is mentioned four times. So is the lark soaring regularly above it. A still more important leitmotif is the stone near the Waldbrunnen, with Juliana or Franz standing on it, shouting verses to the trees.

Besides *Nachkommenschaften* and *Der Waldbrunnen,* Stifter wrote two other stories while he was still working on *Witiko: Der Kuss von Sentze,* first published in the *Gartenlaube für Österreich* in 1866, and *Der fromme Spruch,* written mostly during the summer of 1866, but not published during Stifter's lifetime. In both stories, the older generation of a noble family wants to unite the younger members in marriage, so that the family will not die out and the large estate will not be broken up. In *Der Kuss von Sentze,* two cousins, Erkambert and Walchon, want Erkambert's son Rupert and Walchon's daughter Hiltiburg to marry each other. In *Der fromme Spruch,* Gerlint and her brother Dietwin want the same for their nephew and niece, named after them. Both nephew and niece had been orphaned at an early age and were brought up by their uncle and aunt. In *Der Kuss von Sentze,* the plan seems to fail because—at least on the surface—the young people are repelled rather than attracted by each other. In *Der fromme Spruch,* the uncle and the aunt temporarily believe that the young people love them and not each other. In both stories, the misunderstandings are cleared up. In *Der Kuss von Sentze,* there is quite a change of heart in Hiltiburg. In both stories, the young people find each other, marry, and all ends well.

The reception of the two stories has been no less controversial than that of *Witiko*. Unfortunately, a great deal of commentary on Stifter is completely uncritical. It considers sacrosanct every word Stifter wrote, and sacrilegious the thought of a possible decline of artistic power in the aging, ailing writer. This undiscerning praise has harmed Stifter almost as much as undiscerning blame. One can greatly admire Stifter and yet have the courage to recognize certain weaknesses in his work. Blackall shows this courage and unabashedly calls the two stories failures because of "a jarring dissonance between form and content."[7] The ceremonious style of *Witiko* was transferred to the two stories, especially *Der fromme Spruch*. Dietwin's formal asking for Gerlint's hand in marriage calls to mind Witiko's asking for Bertha's hand. Another example of this overly ceremonious style is the series of birthday greetings in the first chapter, "conveyed in an atmosphere almost like a Papal audience."[8] What in *Witiko* the reader will accept for the twelfth century—although not without difficulty—becomes ludicrous in the nineteenth.

Leo Tepe, the editor of the *Katholische Welt*, had asked Stifter for a contribution. When he received the manuscript of *Der fromme Spruch*, he was disconcerted and consulted two literary men before writing Stifter a long letter of apology for not being able to print the story in his journal. "I ascribe the failure of this story to *Witiko*," he wrote, "because the style of *Der fromme Spruch* reminds one very much of that of *Witiko*. But what pleased in *Witiko* sounds strange and almost ridiculous in our modern age. The endless ceremonies and pompous addresses exchanged between aunt, nephew, niece, and uncle, would certainly supply the critics with ample material for sarcasm."

One of the critics Tepe had consulted is quoted as saying that it was hard to believe that the author was serious and that one was sometimes inclined to take the whole as a caricature of aristocratic families. Stifter defended himself as best he could; he told Tepe that it was true that he wanted to show what was ridiculous in the old-fashioned manners of certain members of the landed gentry, not in a satirical, but rather in a jesting way. The people were still supposed to be "good and honorable."[9] However, this social criticism, of which K. G. Fischer makes a great deal in his edition of *Der fromme Spruch*,[10] is lost on a reader unfamiliar with Stifter's letter to Tepe. More convincing is Stifter's self-defense when he speaks of the young people. Their high-mindedness and great pride, he says, prevent them from taking the first step in declaring their love. But their love should, nevertheless, faintly shine through the whole story.[11]

There are striking similarities between Stifter's *Der fromme Spruch* and Goethe's *Der Mann von fünfzig Jahren,* a *Novelle* inserted in *Wilhelm Meisters Wanderjahre.* In fact, it is very likely that Stifter borrowed from Goethe. In Goethe's *Novelle,* a brother and his sister, simply called the major and the baroness, want their children, Flavio and Hilarie, to marry each other, so that the family estate may not be scattered. But whereas in *Der fromme Spruch,* the uncle, also a man of fifty, deceives himself in thinking that he is loved by his niece, in Goethe's story the niece actually loves the uncle. Flattered by her youthful love, he returns it and intends to marry her. To his father's great relief, his son Flavio is no longer interested in his cousin; he is madly in love with a beautiful, coquettish widow. But she rejects him, and it is during Flavio's ensuing illness and recovery at the baroness's house that the young people discover their mutual love. Father and son closely resemble each other, as do the uncle and his nephew in Stifter's story. Hilarie cannot help seeing in the son a youthful version of the father. The son has had to don his father's clothes, since his own were ruined on his wild flight from the widow's house after her rejection.

As Flavio frees himself more and more from his infatuation with the widow, he is able to see Hilarie's great beauty and grace. The two are gradually drawn to each other. One moonlit night, the father by chance encounters the couple blissfully skating. He has been prepared for such a happening, though not quite consciously so, and is willing to give up Hilarie. Nothing seems to stand in the way of the marriage between Flavio and Hilarie, which, half-jestingly, had been planned from their earliest youth. But Hilarie now declares such a union "improper, even immoral." This brief sketch cannot do justice to either the dramatic action or the subtle psychology of Goethe's *Novelle.* A closer comparison of the two stories reveals how inappropriate Stifter's stylized, abstract form was for such a delicate and psychologically fruitful subject.

Der Kuss von Sentze derives its title from the old custom of asking two hostile members of the noble family of Sentze to exchange a kiss as a means of reconciliation and of preventing further dissension. Communication between members of the family in this story is less ceremonious than in *Der fromme Spruch,* but still too formal to suit modern taste. Though father and son meet at the breakfast table, they still have to arrange a special meeting in the parlor to discuss Rupert's future. The father wants him to marry his cousin Hiltiburg, because they are the last and only descendants of the family. When things go wrong between the young cousins, they are asked to exchange the kiss of reconciliation *(Friedenskuss)*. Rupert, however, recognizes Hiltiburg's kiss as a kiss of love *(Liebeskuss)*. Under cover of darkness, she had secretly kissed him the night he went off to war. He knows now that the unknown girl of that night was Hiltiburg.

The story lacks unity. Our attention should be focused on the two young people and the ambivalence of love as shown in their original hatred and scorn for each other. But we are distracted by a long description of the *Graue Sentze*. This is a house in the woods, which Hiltiburg's father had built for himself as a retreat to which he could retire whenever life disappointed him. He collects various types of moss, because "only nature is absolutely true" and answers "sensibly" if asked "sensibly" (III, 707). It is obvious that Stifter himself speaks here, as we hear him speak when Rupert expounds his views on freedom and the Revolution of 1848 (695). All this is permissible in a novel or a longer *Novelle,* but out of place in this particular short story, the subject of which "is essentially that of an anecdote."[12]

If *Der Kuss von Sentze* and *Der fromme Spruch* may be considered failures, this is not true of Stifter's last work, the so-called *Letzte Mappe*. Much earlier, in 1847, when Stifter was reading proof for the *Studien* version of *Die Mappe,* he had told Heckenast of his plan to expand the story into a book in two volumes. But it was not until 1864, when he was ill and could not work on the demanding *Witiko,* that he went back to *Die Mappe*. He wrote 164 pages of this third version. Unfortunately, we do not possess Heckenast's letters to Stifter. But Heckenast must have become impatient with the poet for not finishing *Witiko* first, as Stifter's answer to a lost letter from him (December 17, 1864) indicates. During his stay in Karlsbad in the spring of 1867, by an immense effort, Stifter finally terminated *Witiko* and was thus free to work once more on *Die Mappe*. But this last, the fourth version, also remained a fragment. "Here the poet died," his friend Aprent wrote at the end of the manuscript. Stifter had prophesied that this would happen when, shortly before his death, he had asked for the manuscript, leafed through it, and then laid it aside.[13]

The *Letzte Mappe*, Stifter's swan song, is a deeply moving work. The poet returns to the scenes of his childhood, youth, and first love. "Thal ob Pirling" is a combination of Oberplan and Friedberg. Other places as well as persons familiar to Stifter in his youth appear in the novel under different names. Matthias Ferent in Pirling is no other than Matthias Greipl in Friedberg; his two daughters Franziska and Josefa are Fanny Greipl and her sister Nanni. At the end of his life, Stifter can look back without pain to this turbulent period of his youth. A wedding, parties, a torchlight procession through the woods—all these are rendered with a light touch. Only once is there a hint at the deep grief which the loss of Fanny had cost him, what could have been if he had married her and if her gentle, black eyes had helped him simply and kindly to live his life (261). The *Letzte Mappe* is Stifter's last hymn of praise to the beauty of his native woods, the simplicity and goodness of their inhabitants, especially the members of his family. Nowhere else in his work has he drawn such a convincing picture of the character of simple country folk, their attachment to age-old customs, their slowness in accepting change, their hospitality, delicacy of feeling, and humility. Their suspicion of anything new reveals itself in their not immediately going to the new doctor—they had never seen a physician. It is fortunate that the beggar Tobias falls ill during a stay at the doctor's house. He is cured and goes around telling people about it. Once they have overcome their suspicion, they put infinite trust in the doctor. But they are unfamiliar with the ways of the world. It does not occur to them that one has to pay for the services of a doctor, as one does for other goods. They have dignity, but are humble and easily embarrassed in the presence of members of a higher social class. They show their natural tact in not asking questions when the doctor is so deeply hurt by the loss of Margarita; they manifest their sympathy through actions.

If, in *Der Nachsommer*, good upbringing prevents people from asking questions, in the *Letzte Mappe* it is the heart that bids people be silent. Even the doctor's sister Anna does not question her brother, but shows her love for him by increased concern for his well-being. She is even willing to sacrifice her own happiness for his sake by indefinitely postponing her marriage with the man she loves.

No one in the family inquires about her reasons. When the doctor's whole family dies during an epidemic, all the people who know him are especially kind to him. The beggar Tobias comes to see him in order to mourn his father's death with him. The two men sit together in the best room of the house, weeping silently. Even within the context of Stifter's work, this scene is incomparable for its utter simplicity and restraint. The description of Soběslaw's death in *Witiko* comes perhaps closest to it. The beggar Tobias is a new figure and does not appear in either the first or the *Studien* version of *Die Mappe*. He is Stifter's special brand of the honest vagabond who can live without a trade, since all people love and help him.[14] His life is easy, and he calls himself "the happiest beggar in the world" (248). He does not live outside society, however, like the zither player Joseph in *Der Nachsommer*. He has more than one function in the widely scattered communities and isolated farms: he is distributor of news, messenger, adviser, comforter, and friend of the children, whose games he directs. A character like Tobias can only flourish in this rural society, where people know each other and depend upon one another.

The descriptions of local customs occupy more space than in the *Studien* version. A wedding, the roofing of the colonel's house *(Lattenschlagen),* where everybody lends a helping hand, and the laying of the foundation stone are described in great detail. The plot also is enlarged. The "Story of the Two Beggars" from the first version—that is, the story of the doctor Augustinus and his friend Eustachius as students in Prague—which Stifter had eliminated in the *Studien* version, is reintroduced. As we can see from the part Stifter finished, Eustachius has become an important figure. As in the first version, he flees from Prague, since he does not have the money to redeem a pledge he had given to a scoundrel. Augustinus sells some of his possessions and pays the pledge. He is unable to find him, however, although he searches diligently and ingeniously. Stifter considerably toned down Augustinus's wild and boisterous student's jargon. He changed little, however, in the passionate letters which Christine, a rich merchant's daughter, writes to Eustachius while he is still in Prague, and which he leaves behind for Augustinus to read. Because of these vestiges of the first version, the novel does not have the unbroken unity of *Der Nachsommer* and *Witiko.*[15] In the last version of *Die Mappe,* in contrast to the first, Augustinus continues his search after he has gone home, but in vain.

The most important change Stifter made in the last version is the elimination of the doctor's intent to hang himself. It is true that, as early as 1847, while he was reading the proofs, Stifter had written to Heckenast that this part had to be eliminated because the doctor would not do such a thing (*Br I,* 209); yet he let it stand. The omission in the novel is in keeping with its calmer tone, but the story is thus deprived of its dramatic climax. We no longer understand why the colonel is so anxious to follow the doctor into the woods, nor does the parallel with the colonel's story hold true any longer. The colonel, too, had tried to kill himself after a disappointment in love.

If the omission of the suicide plan may be considered a weakening of the story, many other changes must be regarded as definite improvements. The events are now told in chronological order. Everything is clear and coherent, and repetitions are avoided. All human relationships are deepened, especially those between the doctor and the colonel and those within the doctor's own family, where the greatest possible tenderness and affection prevail. The doctor's utter loneliness after the loss of his whole family is all the more moving, since it echoes Stifter's loneliness. More space is given to the epidemic which caused the death of the doctor's family, and to his heroic fight against it in spite of his personal grief and weariness. We are reminded of Dr. Rieux's heroic fight—on a larger scale to be sure—in Camus' *La Peste.* Both doctors, moreover, renew their strength through friendship with another man. But Augustinus is still closer in spirit to another physician in French literature, Balzac's doctor in *Le Médecin de campagne,* with whom he shares the epithet "father of the sick" (326). Both men try to combine the work of healing with that of helping people in many other ways. Stifter's doctor helps his fellow men as physician, wealthy man, good neighbor, model farmer, and magistrate. It is more his humanity than his skill as physician which effects a cure in the last patient he treats in the novel. Isabella, the younger daughter of the neighboring Freiherr von Tannberg, suffers from a depression caused by her secret love for the landscape architect Ewald Lind—probably no other than the missing Eustachius. Asked for help, the doctor himself says, *"In diesem Falle wird aber der Mensch mehr als der Arzt leisten können"* (318). (In this case, I shall be more effective as a man than as a physician).

The doctor, very much ahead of his time, uses modern methods of psychotherapy. He tries to distract Isabella from her personal sorrow by showing her the improvements which the colonel and he have initiated. He speaks to her of God's many gifts; he speaks of love and friendship, of the colonel's and his own fate. Finally he dares to mention Eustachius, in whom Isabella immediately sees Lind. She can quietly discuss him with the doctor—a sign that she is cured. She is not jealous of Christine, but wishes to show her friendship and affection, should she ever visit them with Eustachius. Like the doctor, she hopes that they will settle not too far from them. After this talk, Isabella is even more tranquil and cheerful than before. Her parents are told to continue what the doctor has begun, to let Isabella and her sister take on domestic responsibilities and become interested in the world around them. Then, he concludes, the girls can follow their feelings and find the right husbands. At this point the novel ends. There is not much doubt in the reader's mind about a happy ending. *"Es wird sich alles lösen"* (everything will be solved), Isabella had suggested earlier (338). Had Stifter been able to finish the novel, Eustachius would most likely have turned up and gone to Prague to be united with Christine; Margarita would have forgiven the doctor and become his wife, as she does in the first and *Studien* versions. Because of the difference in their social standing, it is doubtful whether Isabella would have married the miller Innozenz, whom she likens to Lind.[16]

In the *Letzte Mappe,* Stifter wrestles, once more, with the problem of fate and the incomprehensibility of the sudden annihilation of the human individual, as he had done in *Abdias* and in the first and second versions of *Die Mappe.* The problem must have been of great importance to him, because he puts the pertinent passage at a very central place now—at the end of the first volume. The new wording is "stylistically superior, because Stifter's thought-progression is much clearer."[17] But the basic philosophy has not changed, even if it is expressed more clearly and less harshly. Fate rides in a golden chariot, crushing whatever is in her way. It does not matter if an individual life is snuffed out prematurely, or if entire nations perish, for others will continue where they have left off. And the grief the individual has brought upon himself and the way he copes with it are of no concern to the *"Allheit"* (deity), which presses on toward its "goal of glory" (250–51).

Neither Stifter nor his critics seem to have realized that there is a dichotomy between this impersonal, aloof deity and the very personal God in whom the characters of the novel believe, the God who governs their lives and answers their prayers. The paragraph, however, closes with a new and more optimistic thought, which is independent of any religious belief. Man is responsible for his sorrow (the doctor clearly speaks here of himself), but he has the power to change and transcend his grief, to sublimate it in his work. He will be rewarded for his change, because something new and extraordinary *(das Ausserordentliche)* will arise from it. As the colonel tells the doctor after the death of the doctor's family, *"Durch den Segen, der aus dem Schmerze in die Taten fliesst, kommt die Erwartung eines Heils, und das Heil erscheint in der Empfindung der Taten"* (From the blessing which flows from our sorrow into our actions comes the expectation of a new happiness, and the new happiness makes itself felt in our awareness of our good deeds) (294).[18]

This idea of sublimating one's grief in one's work and one's caring about others and thus achieving new happiness, could be called the leitmotif of *Die Mappe* and many other of Stifter's works. The colonel and the doctor achieve such sublimation in *Die Mappe,* as do Felix in *Das Haidedorf,* Brigitta and the Major in *Brigitta,* Maria in *Zwei Schwestern,* Hanns in *Der beschriebene Tännling,* and the priest in *Kalkstein.* Throughout Stifter's writing there is infinite trust in the goodness of man and in his power to overcome personal sorrow.

CHAPTER 8

Conclusion

L OOKING back on Stifter's literary career and the praise and criticism it has reaped in more than a century, one is inclined to predict that there will always exist some controversy in the interpretation and evaluation of his works. There will probably never be full agreement as to preference for the earlier or the later writings. At present, scholars seem to be particularly interested in *Witiko* and the *Letzte Mappe*. But there always will be readers who prefer *Der Nachsommer* and the best of the *Novellen*. There will even be some who prefer the first versions of the stories because of their greater spontaneity. It is more than doubtful that Stifter will ever regain the popularity he enjoyed at the time of the publication of his early stories. He will probably remain a writer for Stendhal's "happy few" or for the *"Stillen im Lande"* (the quiet people in the land), as the eighteenth-century pietists were sometimes called. There are great obstacles to securing for Stifter the rank in world literature which his best works deserve. In his *Die Entstehung des Doktor Faustus* Thomas Mann says, "Stifter is one of the most remarkable, profound, quietly bold and curiously fascinating writers of world literature, critically explored far too little."

Stifter is relatively unknown because of the serious lack of translations. He is difficult to translate, and publishers are wary of an author who will never be on the best-seller list. Although Stifter has created such unforgettable figures as Abdias, Brigitta, the uncle in *Der Hagestolz,* and the parson in *Kalkstein,* he does not possess the inexhaustible creative power of a Balzac or a Dickens. This study of Stifter has revealed, as any study of him will, repetitions of motifs, characters, ideas. In the chapter on *Der Nachsommer,* we have mentioned Stifter's refusal to consider any *littérature engagée* and how this fact determines his position in world literature. It makes him less interesting than either Balzac or Dickens for the modern reader and critic, who is often sociologically oriented. Last but not least, it is Stifter's almost complete omission (especially in his later works) of evil, cruelty, extended physical suffering, or mental anguish which turns many modern readers away from him. However, we should not confuse this optimistic outlook with naïveté.

Stifter's optimism was conscious and deliberate: he wanted to show in his work the triumph of moral law. He has been rightly called the most ethical of all German writers of his century. He had the highest possible view of the calling of the artist. He did not tire of reiterating what he thought to be the foremost task of the true artist: to expand the realm of beauty. The beautiful was for him, as we have shown, nothing but the divine in a beautiful garb. Although Stifter's estimate of his own gifts fluctuates and we should perhaps take with a grain of salt his frequent disparagement of the purely artistic merit of his writings, he was sincere in putting their ethical worth above their poetic value.

Stifter believed in the esthetic education of man. Man can be truly human only when his sense of beauty has been developed. To be able to put into his works what was best in himself, to find an echo in kindred spirits—in this, Stifter saw the fulfillment of his life. Nothing could have pleased him more than the fact that Thomas Mann quoted the following passage from Stifter's letters to express his own attitude: "My books are not only poetic creations ..., as moral revelations, as strict and earnest guardians of human dignity, they have a worth that will last longer than their poetic worth in our wretched, frivolous literature."[1] This may seem very out of date to many modern artists. Yet, recent discussions of Jean Genet, Louis-Ferdinand Céline, and the very latest literature of shock, cruelty, and death have made it quite clear that we can no longer evade the question of whether great literature is possible without moral values. Are we willing to renounce our humanity by recognizing as great those writers who glorify war, murder, cruelty, and violence? And although it is true that Stifter's optimistic view of man and nature often does not correspond to reality, it is equally true that the direction in which he asks man to move—toward ever greater rationality, nonviolence and humaneness—seems the only alternative to the primitivistic and suicidal tendencies of our time. Not by accident is Stifter frequently quoted in discussions of a new *Humanität*. In a world of ever increasing noise, pollution, overcrowding, and ugliness, for many a modern man his work also speaks to a deep yearning for solitude, quiet, purity, and beauty.

Notes and References

Chapter One

1. Richard Exner, "Hugo von Hofmannsthal zu Adalbert Stifter," *Adalbert Stifter: Studien und Interpretationen* (Heidelberg: Stiehm, 1968), p. 334. Hereafter referred to as *Studien und Interpretationen.*

2. *Br* refers to *Briefwechsel,* ed. Gustav Wilhelm, Vols. I–VIII=Vols. XVII–XXIV of Adalbert Stifter's *Sämmtliche Werke* (Prague and Reichenberg). See Selected Bibliography.

3. *Br III,* 260: *IV,* 180–81.

4. *Adalbert Stifters Leben und Werk in Briefen und Dokumenten,* ed. K. G. Fischer (Frankfurt: Insel, 1962), p. 679. Hereafter referred to as *Leben und Werk.*

5. Friedrich Gundolf uses the term *Urerlebnis* as contrasted with *Bildungserlebnis* in his book on Goethe.

6. *Br I,* 187: *II,* 246–47: *III,* 111–13.

7. *Br V,* 236–37. For similar statements see Margarete Gump, *Stifters Kunstanschauung* (Berlin: Ebering, 1927), pp. 11–12.

8. For other reasons see Moriz Enzinger, *Adalbert Stifters Bewerbungen um ein Lehramt.* Offprint from *Historisches Jahrbuch der Stadt Linz,* 1967.

9. Story of the two beggars in the first and last versions of *Die Mappe meines Urgrossvaters.* Hereafter referred to as *Die Mappe.*

10. Gustav Wilhelm, *Adalbert Stifters Jugendbriefe,* ed. Moriz Enzinger (Nuremberg: Carl, 1954), pp. 58, 60–62, 66–68. The passage, quoted last, brings to mind the end of Chapter 11 of Part I of Goethe's novel *Die Wahlverwandtschaften.*

11. Her love and care are revealed in the few letters we have from her hand and the unselfish fulfillment of Stifter's innumerable wishes during his long absences from home.

12. When, in 1844, he applied for admission to a pension fund for widows and orphans of painters and sculptors, he spoke of "some small attempts at writing" (*Br I,* 131).

13. For a survey of his rather extensive work see Fritz Novotny, *Adalbert Stifter als Maler* (Vienna: Schroll, 1941).

14. See Christian Otto Arndt, "The Changing Appreciation of the Writings of Adalbert Stifter," Diss., Univ. of Illinois, 1937.

15. "Staatsdinge sind wie eine Blume, die man hegt und wartet, dann wächst sie, die man aber über Nacht durchaus nicht hervorbringen kann"

(VI, 331). Stifter's works are quoted, if not stated otherwise, from *Gesammelte Werke* in sechs Bänden, ed. Max Stefl (Wiesbaden: Insel, 1959).

16. *Br I,* 321. Cf. also the letter to his friend Türck: "das oberste Prinzip steht noch nirgends fest: *dass nehmlich Erziehung die erste und heiligste* Pflicht des Staates ist: denn darum haben wir ja den Staat, dass wir in ihm Menschen seien, und darum muss er uns zu Menschen machen, dass er Staatsbürger habe und ein Staat sei, keine Strafanstalt, in der man immer Kanonen braucht, dass die wilden Thiere nicht losbrechen" (*Br II,* 1).

17. For Stifter and the Revolution, see Hermann Blumenthal, "Adalbert Stifter und die deutsche Revolution von 1848," *Dichtung und Volkstum,* XLI (1941), 211–37; Ruth Brunnhofer-Wartenberg, "Adalbert Stifters Erlebnis und Beurteilung der Revolution von 1848," *Adalbert Stifter-Institut des Landes Oberösterreich, Vierteljahrsschrift,* II (1953), 112–22. Hereafter referred to as *ASILO.* Walter Epping, "Stifters Revolutionserlebnis," *Weimarer Beiträge,* III (1955), 246–60.

18. For details see Otto Jungmair, *Adalbert Stifters Linzer Jahre: Ein Kalendarium* (Nuremberg: Carl, 1958). Cf. also *Br II,* 256–57, 266–67.

19. For Stifter's work as Schulrat see *Die Schulakten Adalbert Stifters,* ed. Kurt Vancsa (Nuremberg: Carl, 1955); Otto Jungmair, *Adalbert Stifters Linzer Jahre* and *Adalbert Stifter und die Schulreform in Oberösterreich nach 1848.* Offprint for das Adalbert Stifter-Institut des Landes Oberösterreich from the *Historisches Jahrbuch der Stadt Linz, 1957.*

20. *Br II,* 75, 139–40, 206–10.

21. Jungmair places a good deal of the blame on the political reaction in Austria.

22. Alois Groszschopf, *Adalbert Stifter: Leben Werk Landschaft.* Zum hundertsten Todestag des Dichters. (Linz: Trauner, 1967), illustrations nos. 150 and 173. Hereafter referred to as Groszschopf.

23. For the latest medical views on his illness and death see: Hermann Wagenbichler, "Adalbert Stifters Todeskrankheit im Spiegel medizinischer Betrachtungen," *Materia Medica Nordmark,* XVII (1965), 780–89; Ernst Kurz, "Adalbert Stifters Krankheiten und Tod," *Münchener Medizinische Wochenschrift,* Volume 108, Heft 21 (May, 1966), pp. 1177–82.

Chapter Two

1. A list of these *Zeitschriften, Almanache, Jahrbücher,* and *Taschenbücher* is to be found in Max Stefl's "Nachwort" to his edition of the *Studien* (II, 696–97). The suggestion that the stories should be published in book form came probably from Stifter himself. Cf. *Br I,* 113, 371.

2. "Auf Schriftstellertum macht das Vorliegende keinen Anspruch, sondern sein Wunsch ist nur, einzelnen Menschen, die ungefähr so denken und fühlen wie ich, eine heitere Stunde zu machen, die dann vielleicht weiter wirkt und irgendein sittlich Schönes fördern hilft."

3. Some of the pros and cons concerning the relative value of the two versions are to be found in Adalbert Stifter, *Erzählungen in der Urfassung* (Augsburg: Kraft, 1950–52), ed. Max Stefl, Vol. I, pp. 361–73. Hereafter referred to as *Urf.* The *Studien* versions will be quoted from the Insel-Verlag edition. See Note 15, Chapter 1.

4. For possible sources of the story see Eric A. Blackall, *Adalbert Stifter* (Cambridge: Univ. Press, 1948), pp. 100–101, and Gerda v. Petrikovits, "Zu Stifters 'Condor,' " *ASILO,* XV (1966), 45–51.

5. Italics are mine.

6. I cannot agree with Gerda v. Petrikovits' interpretation of the story (see note 4) according to which Stifter wanted to depict the fear with which a human being, independent of sex, is seized when confronted with the universe. The phrase "Das Weib erträgt den Himmel nicht," and the fact that both male passengers escape such cosmic fear, seem to contradict her interpretation.

7. A conscious moving away from Jean Paul can be noticed when one compares the *Studien* version with the first redaction. In the first version, Stifter mentions Jean Paul four times (*Urf.* 35, 37, 39, 90). In the *Studien* version, he changes the first reference from "Vater Hans Paul" to "Vater Goethe" (I, 45); the second and third references are altogether omitted; only the fourth remains, where Jean Paul is quoted as "einfältiger Pfarrerssohn aus Baiern" (I, 106). The notes, so typical of Jean Paul's style, are omitted in the *Studien.*

8. "Ich will die unverdient günstige Beurtheilung der 'Feldblumen' in hiesigen Blättern erst zu rechtfertigen suchen, da ich die Fehler der Unruhe und theilweisen Haltlosigkeit, die darin waren, recht gut einsehe . . . Es dünkt mich, der *Hochwald* . . . gehe im milden Redeflusse fort, ein einfach schön Ergiessen, ohne dem koketten Herumspringen, das mich in den Feldblumen ärgert" (*Br I,* 73–74).

9. Actually, *Das Haidedorf* was published before *Feldblumen,* but the *Studien* arrangement is followed, since *Das Haidedorf* is very different in style from *Der Condor* and *Feldblumen* and seems to belong more closely to the following story, *Der Hochwald,* than to the first two *Studien.*

10. "'Meine selbstgewählte Stellung,' sagte er . . . und im tiefen, tiefen Schmerze war es wie eine zuckende Seligkeit, die ihn lohnte" (I, 203–4).

11. *Br I,* 74, 79–80. A few months later, however, in his usual way, Stifter had already become very conscious of the faults of *Der Hochwald* (*Br I,* 104).

12. *Br III,* 223–24, March 7, 1860.

13. *Faust I,* "Wald und Höhle."

14. Hofmannsthal points out that Stifter, in his whole work, never mentions the common poisonous vipers *(Kreuzottern),* native to his Bohemian woods. *Studien und Interpretationen,* pp. 307, 312, 327.

15. "Aber . . . eines Tages wird er fortgehen und ein Held werden, wie sie sagen, das heisst er wird Menschenblut vergiessen, wie die anderen, ohne um den Grund zu fragen, wenn nur Abenteuer und Gefahr dabei ist, und da wird er sich erst gross und würdig dünken" (I, 301).

16. See August Sauer, "Über den Einfluss der nordamerikanischen Literatur auf die deutsche," *Jahrbuch der Grillparzer-Gesellschaft,* XVI (1906), 21–51.

17. See *The Deerslayer,* Chapters XIV, XV, and XXIV.

18. *Ibid.,* Chapters VII and XXVI.

19. See Adalbert Stifter, *Die Scharnast-Erzählungen,* ed. Max Stefl (Königsberg: Gräfe und Unzer, 1942), pp. 425–27.

20. These words call to mind Platen's pessimistic verse: "Denn jeder sucht ein All zu sein, und jeder ist im Grunde nichts."

21. "Die Sonne war über die Waldwand hinunter und warf kühle Schatten auf die Pernitz; im Rücken der Häuser glühten die Felsen, und wie flüssiges Gold schwamm die Luft über all den grünen Waldhäuptern weg. . . . Und immer feierlicher floss die Abenddämmerung . . . immer abendlicher rauschten die Wasser der Pernitz, und immer reizender klangen die Zithern" (I, 338–39 and 438).

22. Theodor Storm greatly admired this part of the *Novelle:* "so muss *in pcto.* der 'Grünen Fichtau' auch jedem, der das gelesen, sein, als wenn ihm für immer ein schönes trauliches Stück Leben geschenkt worden sei." Moriz Enzinger, *Adalbert Stifter im Urteil seiner Zeit* (Vienna: Böhlau, 1968), p. 346.

23. Speaking of the ruins of one of the buildings, Stifter says, "alle die Keuschheit des Marmors war hässlich von Rauch und Flamme geschwärzt und verödet—eine Schicht unreiner Ziegel lag zwischen den beschmutzten Säulen und schändete die edle Leiche des Gebäudes" (I, 399).

24. Blackall, *op. cit.,* p. 143.

25. *Br I,* 209, 212. We possess four versions of it: *Urf.,* 1841/42; *Studien* version 1847; two unfinished versions, of 1864 and 1867, respectively.

26. VI, 130–55; 50–71. Thomas Mann greatly admired "Ein Gang durch die Katakomben." See *ASILO,* XVIII (1969), 40.

27. I, 622. Italics are mine.

28. He does, however, in the last version of *Die Mappe,* which will be treated in a later chapter.

29. "Das ist eine heillose Geschichte. *Das Buch gefällt mir nicht. . . .* Ich wollte drei Karaktere geben, in denen sich die Einfachheit, Grösse und Güte der menschlichen Seele spiegelt, durch lauter gewöhnliche Begebenheiten und Verhältnisse gebothen—wäre es gelungen, dann hätte das Buch mit der Grösse, mit der Einfalt und mit dem Reize der Antike gewirkt.— —So aber ist es nicht so, und es hat mich oft bei der Correctur geradezu *schreklich* gelangweilt. . . . Die ersten 4 Bogen . . . sind so ziemlich gut,

besonders die Erzählung des Obrists, welcher Karakter überhaupt der beste ist, dann muss der Eissturz und manche Scene mit Margarita gut wirken. Das andere——wie wird es sein?! Etwa ist die Heimkehr des Doktors und sein anfängliches Wirken mit Vater und Schwestern rein genug, dann aber kömmt bestimmt eine Leere und Öde" (*Br I*, 208–9).

Chapter Three

1. Something of this objectivity is implied, although not stated, in the short episode with the Jew in *Die Mappe*. The young Augustinus "drags" the Jew *(den Gassenjuden)* into his room and "chases him away" after the bargain is completed. The Jew is dishonest, to be sure, but Augustinus, too, delights in outwitting him in his second dealing with him. Cf. *Urf.*, p. 216; last version, pp. 55, 115–17.

2. Walter Silz shows why it is, nevertheless, a *Novelle* and not a novel. *Realism and Reality* (Chapel Hill: The Univ. of North Carolina Press, 1962), pp. 52–54. See also Benno von Wiese, *Die deutsche Novelle von Goethe bis Kafka,* II (Düsseldorf: Bagel, 1962), pp. 144–45.

3. Deborah's tragic fate is summarized in one moving sentence: "Sie hatte wenig Glück in dieser Ehe gehabt, und als es angefangen hätte, musste sie sterben" (II, 43).

4. An almost identical manifestation of extreme loyalty occurs in *Der Hagestolz,* in the story of the little Pomeranian dog (II, 299–301).

5. "Abdias . . . wollte sich die weissen Haare ausraufen—er heulte—er stiess ungeheure Verwünschungen aus—er lief gegen das Maultier hin und riss die zweite Pistole aus dem Halfter, und krampfte seine Finger darum" (II, 89).

6. Kurt Gerhard Fischer, "Der jüdische Mensch in Stifters Dichtungs-Denken," *ASILO,* XIV (1965), 109–18.

7. *Realism and Reality,* pp. 58–59. Konrad Steffen, in his *Deutungen* (Basel: Birkhäuser, 1955) speaks of the conflict between Stifter's basic melancholy and his will to see things optimistically (p. 92). This conflict had led him in *Die Mappe* to use an equally fallacious metaphor to explain the relation between fate and human responsibility. If the golden wheels of the rolling universe crush us, he says there, God looks on detached, veiled in his cloak, and does not take our bodies away, because it is we who have laid them there. He showed us the wheels but we did not pay attention to them (I, 464).

8. Rudolf Jansen, "Die Quelle des 'Abdias' in den Entwürfen zur 'Scientia Generalis' von G. W. Leibniz?," *ASILO,* XIII (1964), 57–69. Cf. also Eric A. Blackall, *op. cit.,* p. 177, and Hermann Boeschenstein, *Deutsche Gefühlskultur,* II (Berne: Haupt, 1966), p. 60. Werner Kohlschmidt and Kurt Mautz, on the other hand, emphatically deny any causal connection

between guilt and fate in Abdias's life. See Werner Kohlschmidt, *Form und Innerlichkeit* (Berne: Francke, 1955), p. 220; Kurt Mautz, "Das antagonistische Naturbild in Stifters 'Studien,' " *Studien und Interpretationen,* pp. 36–37.

9. Joachim Müller, "Thomas Mann über Adalbert Stifter," *ASILO,* XII (1963), 60 and 61.

10. *German Narrative Prose,* Vol. I, ed. E. J. Engel (London: Wolff, 1965), pp. 111–88.

11. "Neben dem Unterrichte gab er seinem Sohn unversehens auch ein anderes Kleinod mit, . . . nämlich sein eigenes einfältiges, metallstarkes, goldreines Männerherz, welches Hugo unsäglich liebte und unbemerkt in sich sog, so dass er schon als Knabe etwas Eisenfestes und Altkluges an sich hatte, wie ein Obrist des vorigen Jahrhunderts, aber auch noch als Mann von zwanzig Jahren etwas so einsam Unschuldiges, wie es heut zu Tage selbst tief auf dem Lande kaum vierzehnjährige Knaben besitzen" (II, 119–20).

12. Italics are mine.

13. He stresses the *Reinheit* of her clothing, hair, and body (157). And when he speaks of her having surrendered to him, he calls her "das ausserordentlich schöne Weib . . . das ihm unschuldig, treu, willenlos, wie ein liebliches Kind, hingegeben war" (163).

14. "Also könntest du der sogenannten Ehre das warme, ewige, klare Leben opfern?" (179)

15. Werner Hoffmann, "Zur Interpretation und Wertung der ersten Fassung von Adalbert Stifters Novelle 'Das alte Siegel,' " *ASILO,* XV (1966), 80–96; J. P. Stern, "Propitiations: Adalbert Stifter," *Re-interpretations* (London: Thames and Hudson, 1964), p. 262; Eric A. Blackall, "Das alte Siegel," *Studien und Interpretationen,* p. 69.

16. *Brigitta* is very often included in the curriculum of the German Gymnasium (especially in girls' schools) and is therefore fairly well known among German youth.

17. Franz H. Mautner discusses the elements of suspense in his "Randbemerkungen zu 'Brigitta,' " *Studien und Interpretationen,* pp. 89–102.

18. The two vagabonds in his work have a function in society. The one, the zither player Joseph in *Der Nachsommer,* is an accomplished musician; the other, the very dignified and beloved beggar Tobias in the last version of *Die Mappe,* carries out many voluntary tasks.

19. II, 250. In similar words, Margarita in *Die Mappe* says that through her father she had learned what a wonderful man *(herrlicher Mann)* the doctor had become (I, 668).

20. The happy ending of *Brigitta* would seem to be quite essential for the meaning of the story, although a recent study suggests that the modern reader might prefer to omit it. (Gerda v. Petrikovits, "Zur Entstehung der Novelle 'Brigitta,' " *ASILO,* XIV [1965], 104.)

21. "Mit einer Zartheit, mit einer Verehrung, die wie an die Hinneigung zu einem höheren Wesen erinnerte, behandelte der Major das alternde Weib; sie war mit sichtlicher innerlicher Freude darüber erfüllt, und diese Freude, wie eine späte Blume, blühte auf ihrem Antlitze und legte einen Hauch von Schönheit darüber, wie man es kaum glauben sollte" (II, 244).

22. Lunding rightly remarks that Victor is related to the image of "the pure youth" *(Bild des reinen Jünglings)* in the works of Klopstock, Hölderlin, Nietzsche, George and Walter Flex *(op. cit.,* p. 55). To these we should like to add Ernst Penzoldt, a modern writer, sculptor, painter, and admirer of Stifter. This age also fascinated many Renaissance painters.

23. Cf. Margaret Gump, "Zum Problem des Taugenichts," *Deutsche Vierteljahrsschrift für Literaturwissenschaft und Geistesgeschichte,* XXXVII (1963), 542. Stifter's love of dogs also found its expression in *Die Mappe* and *Abdias.*

24. P. 281. Her words call to mind Walther von der Vogelweide's "Owê war sint verswunden alliu mîniu jâr?" and François Villon's "Où sont les neiges d'antan?"

25. Lunding comments on how much attention Stifter paid to "the pathological psychology of loneliness" *(op. cit.,* p. 54).

26. P. 370. The uncle's feeling is almost identical with that of Jodok in *Die Narrenburg,* except that Jodok experiences the uniqueness and transience of one's individual being in spite of having a son.

27. "Der 'Hagestolz selbst' *sollte ein grandios düster prächtiger Karakter werden*" *(Br I,* 122).

28. See Fritz Novotny, *Stifter als Maler,* 3rd edition (1948), plates 21–28, 30–32. One of his best Alpine paintings, *Der Königsee mit dem Watzmann,* is now in the possession of the Austrian Gallery at the Belvedere in Vienna.

29. Similarly, the doctor in J. P. Hebel's "Der geheilte Patient" advises the rich hypochondriac to take long walks, cut wood, and eat with moderation.

30. In the last version of *Die Mappe,* Stifter describes Dr. Augustinus' attempt at curing a mental disturbance. His approach there is psychological and astonishingly modern.

31. For literary models, see Wilhelm Kosch, *Adalbert Stifter und die Romantik,* Prager deutsche Studien, 1 (Prag: Bellmann, 1905), pp. 84–86; *Stifters Werke,* Auswahl in sechs Teilen, ed. Gustav Wilhelm (Leipzig: Bong, 1910), dritter Teil, pp. 18–19.

32. "In all shades of subdued green, gray and blue the marvelous scene stretched forth. Hovering and undulating in the melancholy dusk there appeared panes of color into which the rocks sketched dim quivers of light. Where the land lay bare, nothing but sand and gravel, patches of fawn-colored brightness or softly muted colors showed. In the distance, the hazy outline of a mountain could be perceived, serene and faintly red. . . . Thence

extended two long fiery banks of cloud, kindled by the setting sun and bordered by the pale, dull green of the southern sky, a green that shimmered ever so gently and ran up into flaming blue."

33. "Diese wirklich ausserordentliche Schönheit, und doch etwas Verkommenes darinnen, als flehe die Miene um Abhülfe eines tiefen Übels, das sie hinwelken mache. . . ." (*Urf.*, p. 147). In the *Studien* version, the less stark expression "etwas Verwelkendes und Verblühendes" is used (562). In another passage of the first version (omitted in the *Studien* version) Falkhaus calls Camilla "ein schönes, eingeknicktes, verkommenes Wesen" (*Urf.*, p. 156). For an extended comparison of the two versions, see Werner Hoffmann, *Adalbert Stifters Erzählung "Zwei Schwestern": Ein Vergleich der beiden Fassungen.* Marburger Beiträge zur Germanistik, Vol. XVII (Marburg: Elwert, 1966).

34. This love of collecting, this tendency to transform parts of one's house into a small museum, anticipates *Der Nachsommer.*

35. The colonel, who knows that Augustinus, upset about Margarita's rejection, might commit suicide, asks him whether he had noticed how beautifully the grain was growing this year (I, 468). Victor's foster mother, after he had told her that nothing could give him joy any longer, asks him whether he had not seen that the lettuce at the garden plank had sprouted overnight (II, 268).

36. Lunding, *op. cit.,* p. 66.

37. "Höchst reizvoll ist es nun zu verfolgen, wie die untergründige Dämonie eines leidenschaftlich bewegten Innern niemals zum Durchbruch kommen darf, sondern vielmehr von einer verdeckenden und verhüllenden Wortkunst mit allen Mitteln unterdrückt wird. Das äusserlich Sichtbare, die Handlungen und Bewegungen des betrogenen Hanns, wird sozusagen unter die Zeitlupe gebracht und in seine selbstverständlichen Einzelheiten aufgelöst, wodurch eine starke Stilisierung, deren augenfälligstes Kennzeichen die anaphorische Wiederholung ist, zustande kommt" (Lunding, *op. cit.,* pp. 63–64).

38. Blackall, *Adalbert Stifter,* p. 220.

39. Walther Rehm, "Stifters Erzählung 'Der Waldgänger' als Dichtung der Reue," *Begegnungen und Probleme* (Berne: Francke, 1957), pp. 317–45.

40. "Er tat dies immer, wenn er besonders traulich und freundlich war" (III, 464–65). It is hard to understand how Stern could call those occasions "solemn" (J. P. Stern, *Re-interpretations,* p. 284).

41. Stern calls it "Stifter's finest *Novelle*" (*ibid.,* p. 280).

Chapter Four

1. In a letter to Heckenast (Jan. 9, 1850), Stifter had already expressed the same thought. It seems strange that he uses there the word *Jünglinge* (male youth), as if young girls were not included in the reading public.

156 ADALBERT STIFTER

2. Alfred Doppler, "Adalbert Stifter und Oskar Loerke," *ASILO,* XVI (1967), 31.

3. This epigram appeared three times, 1849, 1851, and 1852, before it finally found a place in Hebbel's collected poems. The first time, it appeared with the subtitle, "to one of them," pointing clearly at Stifter; the second and third time, this subtitle was replaced by "Brockes and Gessner, Stifter, Kompert and so on."

4. For further examples see Ernst Bertram, *Studien zu Adalbert Stifters Novellentechnik,* 2nd edition (Dortmund: Ruhfus, 1966), pp. 59ff.; Fritz Novotny, *op. cit.,* pp. 54ff.

5. Cf. Margarete Gump, *Stifters Kunstanschauung,* pp. 25ff., *Br I,* 214.

6. *Br I,* 214, 240–41, 247ff.; *Br II,* 189–90, 192ff. *Wirkungen eines weissen Mantels, Urf.,* 163–65; *Die Mappe,* I, 449–50, 602; *Der Hagestolz,* II, 258; *Zwei Schwestern,* II, 495; "Der arme Spielmann von Grillparzer," VI, 252–54; "Winterbriefe aus Kirchschlag," VI, 554.

7. Jeremias Gotthelf, *Sämtliche Werke in 24 Bänden,* ed. Rudolf Hunziker und Hans Bloesch (Erlenbach-Zurich: Rentsch, 1921), XI, 347.

8. Stratton Buck, *Gustave Flaubert,* (New York: Twayne, 1966), p. 37.

9. *Br II,* 85; *Erzählungen in der Urfassung,* Vol. III, pp. 344–46.

10. Thomas Mann, *Die Entstehung des Doktor Faustus* (Stockholm: S. Fischer, 1966), p. 101.

11. This little trait shows once more Stifter's preoccupation with this essential commodity of human life, and he has the young girl preach a little sermon on its importance and purity (III, 113–14).

12. In the first version, the protagonist is a Protestant and could have married the girl after becoming a minister.

13. III, 141–43; I, 421ff., 429, 482; II, 375.

14. The basic facts of the story were actually related to Stifter by Antonie Arneth, the wife of his friend, the historian Joseph Arneth.

15. Adalbert Stifter. *Limestone and Other Stories,* trans. and with an Introduction by David Luke (New York: Harcourt, Brace & World, 1968), p. 17.

16. Trans. by David Luke, *ibid.,* p. 105.

17. The story had first appeared as *Der Pförtner im Herrenhause* in *Libussa,* Jahrbuch für 1852. Cf. *Stifters Werke,* ed. Gustav Wilhelm, 4. Teil, pp. 21–24.

18. In Eisenmeier's Stifter Bibliographies of 1964 and 1971, 126 separate editions are listed, the highest number for any single story. Twenty-seven are translations in seven different languages, one of them a transcription into shorthand!

19. *Stifters Werke,* ed. Gustav Wilhelm, 6. Teil, pp. 264–66.

20. *Rock Chrystal: A Christmas Tale,* trans. by Elizabeth Mayer and

Marianne Moore (New York: Random House, rev. ed., 1965). Auden's remark is quoted from the book jacket.

21. Goethe's Mignon has, without doubt, influenced Stifter's *braunes Mädchen.* Cf. especially the end of *Katzensilber* with the end of Chapter 14, Book II of *Wilhelm Meisters Lehrjahre.* But in spite of many similarities, we cannot overlook the fact that Goethe's Mignon is a peerless creation of poetic genius and that none of her literary descendants possesses her unique hold on our imagination and sympathy.

22. III, 249, 251, 281, 282, 293, 316.

23. "Sie ging zu dem Tellerchen Blondköpfchens, tat mit einem Löffel Erdbeeren auf dasselbe, und Blondköpfchen begann zu essen. Sie ging zu dem Tellerchen Schwarzköpfchens, tat Erdbeeren darauf, und Schwarzköpfchen fing an zu essen. Sie ging zu dem Tellerchen Braunköpfchens, tat Erdbeeren darauf, und Braunköpfchen ass sie. Sie ging zu dem Tellerchen des braunen Mädchens, legte Erdbeeren darauf, und das braune Mädchen begann zu essen" (291–92).

24. It is quite obvious that Stifter consciously used the diminutives in order to descend to the level of children. To win the confidence of the strange girl, the mother dresses and wears her hair like her little daughter and thus becomes "ein grosses Schwarzköpfchen" (291).

25. See Lunding, *op. cit.,* p. 61, and Walter Silz, *Realism* and *Reality,* pp. 4–5.

26. Cf. Margaret Gump, "Ernst Penzoldt: Ein Humanist unserer Zeit," *German Quarterly,* XXXIX (1966), 52–53.

27. *Stifters Werke,* ed. Gustav Wilhelm, 4. Teil, pp. 37–38; *Br VII,* 126–27.

28. A. R. Hein, *Adalbert Stifter,* 2nd edition (Vienna: Krieg, 1952), I, 410, II, 929.

Chapter Five

1. Moriz Enzinger, *Adalbert Stifter im Urteil seiner Zeit* (Vienna: Böhlau, 1968), pp. 228–31.

2. "Der Wanderer und sein Schatten," *Menschliches, Allzumenschliches.* Cf. also Nietzsche's letter to Peter Gast, April, 1887: "*In dieser Richtung liegt noch eine ganze Welt der Schönheit.*"

3. Alan Pryce-Jones's review of *Miss MacIntosh, My Darling* by Marguerite Young, *New York Herald Tribune,* Sept. 16, 1965.

4. Alfred Doppler, "Adalbert Stifter and Oskar Loerke," *ASILO,* XVI (1967), 27.

5. Benno Reifenberg, *Der Nachsommer—Der grüne Heinrich.* Freies Deutsches Hochstift, Frankfurt am Main, *Vorträge und Schriften,* hgg. von Ernst Beutler, XIV, 28. In this connection one might also mention Gerhard Uhde's rather mediocre narration, *Das rettende Buch: Eine Be-*

gebenheit, which has for its background the last days of the German occupation of Prague. (Wolfenbüttel: Grenzland, 1965).

6. W. Grabert and A. Mulot, *Geschichte der deutschen Literatur*, 7th edition (Munich: Bayerischer Schulbuchverlag, 1961), p. 327.

7. Victor Lange, "Stifter. Der Nachsommer," *Der deutsche Roman*, ed. Benno von Wiese (Düsseldorf: Bagel, 1963), II, 50.

8. Hugo von Hofmannsthal, "Stifters 'Nachsommer,'" *Ausgewählte Werke in zwei Bänden* (Frankfurt a.M.: Fischer, 1957), II, 692.

9. *Studien und Interpretationen*, p. 293.

10. Cf. Walther Rehm, *Nachsommer* (Munich: Lehnen, 1951), Chapter II.

11. *Br IV*, 273. Cf. also *Br IV*, 267 and *Br V*, 193. Heckenast published a shortened edition in one volume in 1877. This version was several times republished by Heckenast's successor Amelang—without receiving much attention, however (IV, 864).

12. See pp. 241, 267, 472.

13. See pp. 749–50, 759, 764–66, 773, 785.

14. For a summary of the rose motif and its symbolic function, see Christine Oertel Sjögren, "Mathilde and the Roses in Stifter's *Nachsommer*," *PMLA*, LXXXI (1966), 400–08.

15. For a picture see Groszschopf, No. 172. Reading Stifter's description, one would rather think of an earlier work, such as Myron's Athena.

16. The German word *edel*, which Stifter uses here, is well-nigh untranslatable, because it has the meaning of the Greek *eugenes*, i.e., people born with a noble disposition.

17. For Stifter's relation to antiquity, see Margarete Gump, *Stifters Kunstanschauung*, pp. 40–48.

18. Margaret Gump, "Ernst Penzoldt: Ein Humanist unserer Zeit," *The German Quarterly*, XXXIX (1966), 46.

19. See Groszschopf, Nos. 60/61.

20. Horst Albert Glaser, *Die Restauration des Schönen: Stifters "Nachsommer"* (Stuttgart: Metzler, 1965), p. 43.

21. "Parce que les gens de condition libre, bien nés, bien instruits, conversant en compagnies honnêtes, ont par nature un instinct et aiguillon qui les pousse toujours à des faits vertueux, et les retire du vice; ils le nomment honneur."

22. The spiritual kinship between Humboldt's *Briefe an eine Freundin* and *Der Nachsommer* was quickly discovered by Stifter research. It is not accidental that Stifter included so many passages by Wilhelm von Humboldt in his *Lesebuch zur Förderung humaner Bildung*. These passages probably would have had little appeal to youth, had the book been accepted by the Ministry of Education.

23. See pp. 691–93, 855–56, 858–59. For Roland, see Christine Oertel Sjögren, "The Monstrous Painting in Stifter's *Der Nachsommer*," *JEGP*,

LXVIII (1969), 92–99; for the zither player, see her "Stifter's Affirmation of Formlessness in *Nachsommer*," *Modern Language Quarterly,* XXIX (1968), 407–14.

24. The passage is hard to translate, because the German adjectives "rein" and "hold" have a strong spiritual as well as physical implication.

25. Benno Reifenberg, *op. cit.*, p. 17.

26. This expression, so characteristic of Stifter, can only be understood in this context if we know that the word *Dinge* for Stifter means objects as well as affairs, situations. For the almost unlimited use of the word *Ding* in Stifter's work, see Karl Josef Hahn, *Adalbert Stifter: Religiöses Bewusstsein und dichterisches Werk* (Halle a.d. Saale: Akad. Verlag, 1938), pp. 68–102; Wilhelm Dehn, *Ding und Vernunft: Zur Interpretation von Stifters Dichtung* (Bonn: Bouvier, 1969), Chapter II, "Der Ding-Begriff und Stifters Sprachgebrauch."

27. For the furniture, see Groszschopf, Nos. 150 and 173; for the Kefermarkt Altar, No. 163.

28. *Leben und Werk,* pp. 444–45. Ar ėlie von Handel makes the interesting remark that in her opinion Stifter's love of cacti complemented a vein of softness in his character.

29. Blackall thinks that the influence has been overrated. *Adalbert Stifter,* pp. 318–19.

30. See Note No. 3.

31. See *Br III,* 188–89, 194, 217–18.

32. Arno Schmidt, "Der sanfte Unmensch: Einhundert Jahre Nachsommer," in *Dya na Sore: Gespräche in einer Bibliothek* (Karlsruhe: Stahlberg, 1958), pp. 194–229. For Glaser, see Note 20.

33. "Ich habe wahrscheinlich das Werk der Schlechtigkeit willen gemacht, die im Allgemeinen mit einigen Ausnahmen in den Staatsverhältnissen der Welt in dem sittlichen Leben derselben und in der Dichtkunst herrscht. Ich habe eine grosse einfache sittliche Kraft der elenden Verkommenheit gegenüber stellen wollen" (To Heckenast, Feb. 11, 1858, *Br III,* 93).

34. Glaser, *op. cit.*, p. 59.

35. *Ibid.,* p. 56. Moriz Enzinger, *Adalbert Stifter im Urteil seiner Zeit,* pp. 218 and 339.

36. "Ich hoffe hiemit etwas zu 'dichten' nicht zu 'machen.' Die ganze Lage so wie die Karaktere der Menschen sollen nach meiner Meinung etwas Höheres sein, das den Leser über das gewöhnliche Leben hinaus hebt, und ihm einen Ton gibt, in dem er sich als Mensch reiner und grösser empfindet. . . ." (To Heckenast, Feb. 29, 1856, *Br II,* 297–98).

37. Only when he began work on the novel, did he speak of it as *"socialer Roman"* (May 4, 1853, *Br II,* 147). Subsequently, he changed the subtitle "Eine Erzählung aus unseren Tagen" to "Eine Erzählung." (March 22, 1857, *Br III,* 14.)

38. Konrad Steffen, *Adalbert Stifter: Deutungen,* pp. 221–27.

39. "Dieses tiefere Leben soll getragen sein durch die irdischen Grund-
lagen bürgerlicher Geschäfte der Landwirthschaft des Gemeinnuzens und
der Wissenschaft und dann der überirdischen der Kunst der Sitte und *eines
Blikes, der von reiner Menschlichkeit geleitet, oder wenn Sie wollen, von
Religion geführt höher geht als blos nach eigentlichen Geschäften* (welche
ihm allerdings Mittel sind) Staatsumwälzungen und andern Kräften, welche
das mechanische Leben treiben." (Feb. 11, 1858, *Br III*, 94). Italics are mine.

40. These are the last lines of a short poem Goethe wrote in a copy of his
Iphigenie, which he sent to the actor Krüger in 1827.

41. Charles Baudelaire, *Fleurs du mal,* "Invitation au voyage."

42. See Note 4.

Chapter Six

1. We arrive at twenty years by including Stifter's plans for historical
novels, which already contained material to be used later in *Witiko.* For
a detailed account of the origin of, and work on, *Witiko,* see Karl Flöring,
Die historischen Elemente in Adalbert Stifters "Witiko", Giessener
Beiträge zur Deutschen Philologie, No. 5 (Giessen, 1922), pp. 5–17.

2. Lunding, *op. cit.,* p. 88; Franz Hüller, *Adalbert Stifters "Witiko":
Eine Deutung* (Nuremberg: Carl, 1953), pp. 85–86.

3. Twenty-eight years after the publication of his epoch-making Stifter
biography, Hein regretted his harsh appraisal of *Witiko.* See 2nd edition,
II, 962.

4. Friedrich Gundolf, *Adalbert Stifter* (Burg Giebichenstein: Werkstätten der Stadt Halle, 1931), p. 66.

5. Hermann Hesse, *Gesammelte Werke* (Frankfurt: Suhrkamp, 1970),
XII, 282. Stifter himself wrote to Heckenast on June 8, 1861, "The so-called
historical novel seems to me to be the epic in prose" (*Br III,* 282).

6. The word *Langeweile* is hard to translate. Although it is generally
rendered by boredom, tediousness, it literally means a long time and is the
opposite to *Kurzweil,* a short time, meaning any amusing pastime.

7. For Thomas Mann's views on *Witiko* see Thomas Mann, *Briefe 1937–
1947,* ed. Erika Mann (Frankfurt: S. Fischer, 1963), p. 458, and Joachim
Müller, "Thomas Mann über Adalbert Stifter," *ASILO,* XII (1963), 62.

8. *Limestone and Other Stories,* p. 29.

9. Margaret Gump, "Das Goethejahr 1949," *DVLG,* XXV (1951), 493.

10. Hüller points out that Stifter thus purposely evades the question of
Witiko's nationality, that is, whether he is German or Czech. *Op. cit.,* p. 60.

11. "'Hoher Herr,' antwortete Witiko, 'ich bin zu dir gegangen, weil ich
dich für den rechtmässigen Herzog hielt, ich habe dir dann mit Freude ge-
dient, weil du ein guter Herzog bist, und ich habe Liebe für dich gewonnen,
weil du ein rechter Mann bist'" (678).

12. The destruction of the Witikohaus is recounted in the earlier *Novelle,
Der Hochwald.*

13. Cf. Preface to *Bunte Steine* and letters to Heckenast, July 17, 1844, April 10, 1860, June 8, 1861. (*Br I*, 124, *Br III*, 231, 282.)

14. *Zeitschrift für deutsche Philologie*, LXI (1936), 398–402; 407.

15. Lunding, *op. cit.*, p. 94. Max Rychner, *Welt im Wort* (Zurich: Manesse-Verlag, 1949), p. 203. Cf. also p. 197.

16. In an interview with a reporter, Brig. Gen. Sidney B. Berry, Jr., said of his soldiers, "God bless them all. God protect them all. And God take to heaven all those who don't make it through" (*Life*, Sept. 25, 1970, p. 62).

17. Stifter himself, however, in his short article, "Dankfest aus Anlass der Beendigung des Aufstandes in Ungarn," spoke of the grave afflictions God had sent Austria.

18. How much more shocking are Grimmelshausen's *Der abenteuerliche Simplizissimus* (Thirty Years War), Remarque's *Im Westen nichts Neues* (First World War), Penzoldt's *Zugänge* (Second World War), to mention some war fiction written from the author's bitter personal experience.

19. Konrad Steffen, *Deutungen*, pp. 245–46.

20. Hüller, *op. cit.*, pp. 63ff. Neither can we subscribe to Grolman's statement: "Es macht gar keinen grossen Unterschied, dass Gottfried Keller eine ideale Demokratie erkämpft [in *Martin Salander*] und Stifter eine hierarchisch-patriachalische Monarchie ständischen Gepräges zeigt; denn es kommt allenthalben doch wohl darauf an, was der Mensch aus den der Vokabel zugrunde liegenden Wirklichkeiten macht. . . ." Adolf von Grolman, *Adalbert Stifters Romane* (Halle/Saale: Niemeyer, 1926) pp. 93–94.

21. Moriz Enzinger, *Adalbert Stifter im Urteil seiner Zeit*, p. 341.

22. In German, only the word *Dinge* is used; the dialogue is thus much more effective. For the use of the word *Ding* in Stifter's work see Chapter 5, Note 26.

23. Georg Weippert, *Stifters Witiko: Vom Wesen des Politischen* (Munich: Oldenbourg, 1967), pp. 183ff.

24. *Op. cit.*, p. 95.

25. *Maximen und Reflexionen*, zweite Abteilung.

26. Max Rychner, *Welt im Wort*, p. 186.

27. One's taste, according to Lunding, who refers to the work of the art historian Wilhelm Worringer, is determined by one's relation to these two polar types of art: *Abstraktion und Einfühlung* (abstract, stylized art and organic art, art of empathy). *Op. cit.*, pp. 97ff.

Chapter Seven

1. *Br I*, pp. 65 and 69–71.

2. III, 602–03 and *Br II*, 249.

3. *Adalbert Stifter*, pp. 344–45.

4. III, 606–07. In *Der Nachsommer*, Heinrich says, "Wem das nicht

heilig ist, was ist, wie wird er Besseres erschaffen können, als was Gott erschaffen hat?" (337) And in the essay "Über Kunst" Stifter says, "Realismus (Gegenständlichkeit) wird so gerne geradehin verdammt. Aber ist nicht
Gott in seiner Welt am allerrealsten?" (VI, 446). The dichotomy between
realism and idealism is dissolved in the work of the true artist who imparts
the divine within himself to every work he creates. (Cf. Margarete Gump,
Stifters Kunstanschauung, pp. 28ff.) The debate about realism versus idealism
is of little or no interest to the modern artist. He will, however, be very
much interested in a surprisingly modern remark about the possibility of
abstract art in Stifter's famous essay, "Die Sonnenfinsternis am 8. Juli
1842." After having felt the sublime music of light and color in this over-
whelming spectacle, Stifter asks himself whether the artist could not create
a "music for the eye" by way of simultaneous and successive lights and
colors, not attached to any concrete object (VI, 594–95).

5. Book V, Chapter 16, end. "Don't ask me to talk, ask me to be silent,/
For I am bound by my secret:/ I should like to show you my very heart,/
but fate will not have it so." The change in the German verse, here, from
"ist mir Pflicht," to "ist eine Pflicht," is insignificant; it may be just a lapse
of memory on Stifter's part.

6. Stifter had never been on the Rigi, or in Switzerland for that matter,
either with fellow students or his wife.

7. *Adalbert Stifter*, p. 349.

8. *Ibid.*

9. For the correspondence between Stifter and Tepe, see *Der fromme
Spruch*, in the first version, ed. K. G. Fischer (Frankfurt: Insel-Verlag,
1962), pp. 92–114.

10. *Ibid.*, pp. 127ff.

11. *Ibid.*, p. 104.

12. Blackall, *Adalbert Stifter*, p. 349.

13. Adalbert Stifter, *Die Mappe meines Urgrossvaters*. Letzte Fassung,
ed. Franz Hüller (Nuremberg: Carl, 1956), p. 342. All page numbers refer
to this edition.

14. For the vagabond theme in the nineteenth- and twentieth-century
literature, see Margaret Gump, "Zum Problem des Taugenichts," *DVLG*,
XXXVII (1963), 529–57.

15. For a detailed account of the changes made in the "Story of the Two
Beggars," see Hermann Kunisch, *Adalbert Stifter, Mensch und Wirklichkeit: Studien zu seinem klassischen Stil* (Berlin: Duncker & Humblot, 1950),
pp. 62ff.

16. Blackall suggests it as a possible solution (*Adalbert Stifter*, p. 419).
He calls Innozenz Anna's widowed husband, but she died before he could
marry her.

17. *Ibid.*, p. 414.

18. After the doctor has performed a very dangerous operation, he says, "Ich aber hatte nun den schönen Wald wieder, der mir bisher gleichsam verfinstert gewesen war. In mein Herz kam eine Freude, wie ich nie geahnt hatte, dass ich eine solche Freude noch auf Erden zu empfinden vermöchte" (311).

Chapter Eight

1. Thomas Mann to Ernst Bertram, Dec. 25, 1917. The quotation is taken from Stifter's letter to Joseph Türck, Feb. 22, 1850. Mann also uses the same quotation in *Betrachtungen eines Unpolitischen* (p. 201) and in a letter to his brother Heinrich (Jan. 3, 1918 or 1919—different sources give these two different dates): in both quotations he omits the phrase "in our wretched, frivolous literature." There is also a brief reference to the quotation in Thomas Mann's letter to Paul Amann, July 11, 1918.

Selected Bibliography

Note: A complete bibliography on Adalbert Stifter has been compiled by Eduard Eisenmeier in his *Adalbert Stifter Bibliography* and *Adalbert Stifter Bibliography, I. Fortsetzung,* Schriftenreihe des Adalbert Stifter-Institutes des Landes Oberösterreich, vols. XXI and XXVI. Linz: Oberösterreichischer Landesverlag, 1964 and 1971. For later publications see *Adalbert Stifter-Institut des Landes Oberösterreich, Vierteljahrsschrift* (abbreviated: *ASILO* or *VASILO*). The standard, scholarly edition of Stifter's works and letters, the Prague-Reichenberg edition, has been out of print for quite some time. A reprint has recently been announced by the publisher Dr. H. A. Gerstenberg, Hildesheim. Strong scientific objections to this reprint have been raised by Helmut Bergner in his article "Zur Ankündigung eines Reprints der Prag-Reichenberger Stifter-Ausgabe," *ASILO,* XXI (1972), 49–51. In the same issue the preparation of a new, complete, historical-critical edition of Stifter's works and letters was announced.

PRIMARY SOURCES

A. Stifter's Works and Letters

Sämmtliche Werke. (In the series entitled *Bibliothek deutscher Schriftsteller aus Böhmen,* later *aus Böhmen, Mähren und Schlesien.*) Prague: J. G. Calve, 1901 ff.; Reichenberg: F. Kraus, 1927 ff. For details see no. 227 in Eisenmeier's bibliography and the note above. For the present study, mainly the volumes containing Stifter's correspondence have been used, i.e., vols. XVII–XXIV, referred to as *Briefwechsel (Br)* I–VIII. For vol. XIX *(Br III),* the second edition of 1929 has been used.

Gesammelte Werke, ed. Max Stefl. 6 vols. Wiesbaden: Insel-Verlag, 1959. All quotations in this study, if not otherwise indicated, are from this edition.

Gesammelte Werke, ed. Max Stefl. Darmstadt: Wissenschaftliche Buchgemeinschaft (n.d.). 9 vols. Includes first versions.

Werke. Selection in six parts, ed. Gustav Wilhelm. Berlin, Leipzig, Vienna, Stuttgart: Bong, 1910. Does not include *Witiko* and has only two sections from *Der Nachsommer,* but the introductions and annotations to the different parts are still very valuable.

Erzählungen in der Urfassung, ed. Max Stefl. 3 vols. Augsburg: Kraft, 1950–1952.

Julius. Eine Erzählung, ed. Kurt Gerhard Fischer. Linz: Oberösterreichischer Landesverlag, 1965. Schriftenreihe des Adalbert StifterInstitutes des Landes Oberösterreich, vol. XXII. Hereafter referred to as Schriftenreihe d. Ad. Stifter-Inst.

Die Mappe meines Urgrossvaters. Letzte Fassung, ed. Franz Hüller. Nuremberg: Carl, 1956.

Der fromme Spruch. Erzählung. First version, published for the first time by K. G. Fischer. Frankfurt: Insel-Verlag, 1962. Insel-Bücherei No. 767.

"Unbekannte Jugendgedichte Adalbert Stifters," published by Heinrich Micko. *Euphorion,* XXXI (1930), 143–74.

Adalbert Stifters früheste Dichtungen, published for the first time by Heinrich Micko. Prague: Gesellschaft deutscher Bücherfreunde in Böhmen, 1937.

Adalbert Stifters Jugendbriefe. Selected by Gustav Wilhelm. Published posthumously with additions and introduction by Moriz Enzinger. Graz: Stiasny; Nuremberg: Carl, 1954. Schriftenreihe d. Ad. StifterInst., vol. VI.

Adalbert Stifters Leben und Werk in Briefen und Dokumenten. Selection and Preface by K. G. Fischer. Frankfurt: Insel-Verlag, 1962. Wellchosen materials.

B. English Translations

Brigitta, tr. Hermann Saliger. In *Nineteenth-Century German Tales,* ed. Angel Flores. New York: Ungar. Originally, New York: Garden City (Doubleday), 1959.

Brigitta, tr. Ilsa Barea. In *Great German Short Stories,* ed. Stephen Spender. New York: Dell, 1960.

Rock Crystal (Bergkristall), German and English, tr. Harry Steinhauer. In *German Stories/Deutsche Novellen,* a Bantam Dual-Language Book. New York: Bantam Books, 1961.

Rock Crystal: A Christmas Tale, tr. Elizabeth Mayer and Marianne Moore. Illustrated by Josef Scharl. New York: Pantheon Books, 1945. Rev. ed. 1965.

Abdias, tr. N. C. Wormleighton and H. Mayer. In *German Narrative Prose,* Vol. I, ed. E. J. Engel. London: Wolff, 1965.

Limestone and Other Stories. Translated and with an Introduction by David Luke. Contains *Limestone (Kalkstein), Tourmaline (Turmalin), The Recluse (Der Hagestolz).* A Helen and Kurt Wolff Book. New York: Harcourt Brace, 1968.

The Recluse, tr. David Luke. London: Cape, 1968.

For older translations see Bayard Quincy Morgan, *A Critical Bibliography of German Literature in Translation: 1481–1927.* Second edition, and the *Supplement Embracing the Years 1928–1955*. New York and London: The Scarecrow Press, 1965.

The translations in this study, if not otherwise indicated, are my own.

C. Writings related to Stifter's activity as *Schulrat*

Adalbert Stifter and J. Aprent. *Lesebuch zur Förderung humaner Bildung.* Faksimile-Druck, dazu die Briefe Stifters zum Lesebuch, ed. Max Stefl. Munich and Berlin: R. Oldenbourg, 1938. (Schriften der Corona XVIII.)

Die Schulakten Adalbert Stifters. Mit einem Anhang (Personalakten, Organisations-Entwurf der Linzer Realschule). Ed. Kurt Vancsa. Graz: Stiasny; Nuremberg: Carl, 1955. (Schriftenreihe d. Ad. Stifter-Inst., vol. VIII.)

SECONDARY SOURCES

BAHR, HERMANN. *Adalbert Stifter: Eine Entdeckung.* Zurich, Leipzig, Vienna: Amalthea-Verlag, 1919.

———. "Stifter," *Die Neue Rundschau* XXXIII *(1922), 470–487.*

BARNES, H. G. "The Function of Conversations and Speeches in *Witiko.*" In *German Studies presented to Prof. H. G. Fiedler.* Oxford: Clarendon Press, 1938. (Reprint 1969.) Helpful for a better understanding of *Witiko.*

BERTRAM, ERNST. *Studien zu Adalbert Stifters Novellentechnik.* Dortmund: Ruhfus, 1907. Second edition, 1966.

———. *Georg Christoph Lichtenberg. Adalbert Stifter.* Zwei Vorträge. Bonn: Cohen, 1919.

———. "Adalbert Stifter." In *Möglichkeiten: Ein Vermächtnis.* Pfullingen: Neske, 1958, pp. 67–90.

———. "Nietzsche, die Briefe Stifters lesend." Ibid., pp. 201–21.

BINDTNER, JOSEF. *Adalbert Stifter: Sein Leben und sein Werk.* Vienna, Prague, Leipzig: Strache, 1928.

BLACKALL, ERIC A. *Adalbert Stifter: A Critical Study.* Cambridge: University Press, 1948. A fine, scholarly study of Stifter's life and work. Great wealth of background material. Quotations are in German.

BLUMENTHAL, HERMANN. "Adalbert Stifters Verhältnis zur Geschichte," *Euphorion,* XXXIV (1933), 72–110.

———. "Stifters 'Witiko' und die geschichtliche Welt," *Zeitschrift für deutsche Philologie,* LXI (1936), 393–431.

———. "Adalbert Stifter und die deutsche Revolution von 1848," *Dichtung und Volkstum,* XLI (1941), 211–37.

BRUNNHOFER-WARTENBERG, RUTH. "Adalbert Stifters Erlebnis und Beurteilung der Revolution von 1848," *ASILO,* II (1953), 112–22.

DEHN, WILHELM. *Ding und Vernunft: Zur Interpretation von Stifters Dichtung (Literatur und Wirklichkeit,* Bd. 3). Bonn: H. Bouvier & Co., 1969.

DOPPLER, ALFRED. "Adalbert Stifter und Oskar Loerke: Ein Beitrag zur Wirkungsgeschichte Stifters," *ASILO,* XVI (1967), 25–32.

ENZINGER, MORIZ. *Adalbert Stifters Studienjahre (1818–1830).* Innsbruck: Österreichische Verlagsanstalt, 1950.

—————. "Adalbert Stifters Bewerbungen um ein Lehramt." Sonderdruck aus *Historisches Jahrbuch der Stadt Linz 1967.*

—————. *Adalbert Stifter im Urteil seiner Zeit: Festgabe zum 28. Jänner 1968* (Österreichische Akademie der Wissenschaften, Philosophisch-Historische Klasse, *Sitzungsberichte,* 256. Bd.). Vienna: Böhlau Nachf., 1968.

EPPING, WALTER. "Stifters Revolutionserlebnis," *Weimarer Beiträge,* III (1955), 246–60.

FISCHER, KURT GERHARD. *Adalbert Stifter: Psychologische Beiträge zur Biographie. ASILO,* X (1961), 1–112. (=Schriftenreihe d. Ad. Stifter-Inst., vol XVI). Interesting study. Re-examination and re-evaluation of many primary and secondary sources.

FLÖRING, KARL. *Die historischen Elemente in Adalbert Stifters "Witiko."* (Giessener Beiträge zur Deutschen Philologie, No. 5.) Giessen 1922.

GLASER, HORST ALBERT. *Die Restauration des Schönen: Stifters "Nachsommer."* Stuttgart: J. B. Metzler, 1965. One-sided sociological approach.

GROSZSCHOPF, ALOIS. *Adalbert Stifter: Leben. Werk. Landschaft.* Zum hundertsten Todestag des Dichters. Linz: Trauner, 1967. Beautifully illustrated, highly informative book.

GUMP, MARGARETE. *Stifters Kunstanschauung.* Berlin, Ebering, 1927.

GUNDOLF, FRIEDRICH. *Adalbert Stifter.* Burg Giebichenstein: Werkstätten der Stadt Halle, 1931. Some astute observations. On the whole, far too negative. Written partly as a protest against what Gundolf considered a gross overrating of Stifter's work.

HAHN, KARL JOSEF. *Adalbert Stifter: Religiöses Bewusstsein und dichterisches Werk.* Halle: Akademischer Verlag, 1938.

HALLMORE, G. JOYCE. "The Symbolism of the Marble Muse in Stifter's *Nachsommer,"* *PMLA,* LXXIV (1959), 398–405.

HEIN, ALOIS RAIMUND. *Adalbert Stifter: Sein Leben und seine Werke.* 2nd ed., 2 vols., ed. Walter Krieg. Vienna, Bad Bocklet, Zurich: Krieg, 1952. (1st ed. in 1 vol., Prague, 1904.) Still the most extensive biography of Stifter. Written with great empathy. Contains summaries of the individual works. The appendix, containing emendations and additions by Otto Jungmair, is especially valuable.

HOHENSTEIN, LILY. *Adalbert Stifter: Lebensgeschichte eines Überwinders.* Bonn: Athenäum, 1952.

HÜLLER, FRANZ. *Adalbert Stifters "Witiko": Eine Deutung.* (Schriften-reihe d. Ad. Stifter-Inst., vol. V.) Nuremberg: Carl, 1953.

JUNGMAIR, OTTO. *Adalbert Stifter und die Schulreform in Oberösterreich nach 1848.* Sonderdruck für das Ad. Stifter-Inst. d. Landes Ob.-Österr. aus dem "Historischen Jahrbuch der Stadt Linz 1957."

————. *Adalbert Stifters Linzer Jahre:* Ein Kalendarium. (Schriftenreihe d. Ad. Stifter-Inst., vol. VII.) Nuremberg: Carl, 1958. Indispensible tool for any Stifter biographer.

KOHLSCHMIDT, WERNER. "Leben und Tod in Stifters *Studien,*" in *Form und Innerlichkeit.* Berne: Francke, 1955, pp. 210–32.

KUNISCH, HERMANN. *Adalbert Stifter: Mensch und Wirklichkeit: Studien zu seinem klassischen Stil.* Berlin: Duncker & Humblot, [1950]. Deals mainly with the different versions of *Die Mappe meines Urgrossvaters.*

LANGE, VICTOR. "Stifter. Der Nachsommer." In *Der deutsche Roman,* ed. Benno von Wiese. Düsseldorf: Bagel, 1963, II, 34–75.

LUNDING, ERIK. *Adalbert Stifter.* Mit einem Anhang über Kierkegaard und die existentielle Literaturwissenschaft. (=Studien zur Kunst und Existenz, Vol. I.) Copenhagen: Nyt Nordisk Forlag, 1946. Probably the most stimulating book about Stifter.

————. "Forschungsbericht. Probleme und Ergebnisse der Stifterforschung 1945–1954." *Euphorion,* XLIX (1955), 203–44. Valuable guide in the jungle of literature on Stifter.

MÜLLER, JOACHIM. *Adalbert Stifter: Weltbild und Dichtung.* Halle: Niemeyer, 1956.

————. "Thomas Mann über Adalbert Stifter," *ASILO,* XII (1963), 60–63.

NOVOTNY, FRITZ. *Adalbert Stifter als Maler.* Vienna: Schroll & Co., 1941. 3rd ed., enlarged, 1948. Comprehensive study of Stifter's drawings and paintings and their relationship to his writing.

REHM, WALTHER. *Nachsommer: Zur Deutung von Stifters Dichtung.* Berne: Francke; Munich: Lehnen, 1951.

————. "Stifters Erzählung 'Der Waldgänger' als Dichtung der Reue," in *Begegnungen und Probleme: Studien zur deutschen Literaturgeschichte.* Berne: Francke, 1957, pp. 317–45.

ROEDL, URBAN [Bruno Adler]. *Adalbert Stifter. Lebensweg in Bildern.* Munich and Berlin: Deutscher Kunstverlag, [1955].

————. *Adalbert Stifter: Geschichte seines Lebens.* 2nd ed., rev. Berne, Francke, 1958. (1st ed., Berlin: Rowohlt, 1936.)

————. *Adalbert Stifter in Selbstzeugnissen und Bilddokumenten.* Reinbek: Rowohlt, 1965. (=rowohlts monographien, rororo 86.) Very good introduction to Stifter's life and work. Richly illustrated. Extensive bibliography.

RYCHNER, MAX. "Stifters 'Nachsommer.'" In *Welt im Wort. Literarische Aufsätze.* Zurich: Manesse, 1949, pp. 157–80.

———. "Witiko." *Ibid.,* pp. 181–210.

SILZ, WALTER. "Stifter, *Abdias* (1842)." In *Realism and Reality: Studies in the German Novelle of Poetic Realism* (=University of North Carolina Studies in the Germanic Languages and Literatures, No. 11.) Chapel Hill: The Univ. of North Carolina Press, 1962, pp. 52–66; 159–60.

SJÖGREN, CHRISTINE OERTEL. "Isolation and Death in Stifter's *Nachsommer*," *PMLA,* LXXX (1965), 254–58.

———."Mathilde and the Roses in Stifter's *Nachsommer*," *PMLA,* LXXXI (1966), 400–408.

———. "The Cereus Peruvianus in Stifter's *Nachsommer:* Illustration of a Gestalt," *The German Quarterly,* XL (1967), 664–72.

———. "Stifter's Affirmation of Formlessness in *Nachsommer*," *Modern Language Quarterly,* XXIX (1968), 407–14.

———."The Monstrous Painting in Stifter's *Der Nachsommer*," *JEGP,* LXVIII (1969), 92–99.

———. "The Equivocal Light of the Marmorsaal: Traces of Mysticism in Stifter's Novel, *Der Nachsommer*," *JEGP,* LXIX (1970), 108–17.

SPALDING, KEITH. "Adalbert Stifter." In *German Men of Letters.* Vol. V. N. Y. Dufour Editions, 1969, pp. 183–206.

STEFFEN, KONRAD. *Deutungen.* Basel and Stuttgart: Birkhäuser, 1955.

STERN, J. P. "Propitiations: Adalbert Stifter." In *Re-interpretations: Seven Studies in Nineteenth-Century German Literature.* London: Thames and Hudson, 1964, pp. 239–300. Sensitive study of Stifter's life and some major works. Quotations are in German and English.

———. "On Some Criticisms of Stifter's Work." *Ibid.,* pp. 358–62. Examines the critical trends in Stifter studies from the time of Stifter's death to 1961.

STIEHM, LOTHAR, ed. *Adalbert Stifter: Studien und Interpretationen.* Gedenkschrift zum 100. Todestage. Heidelberg: Stiehm, 1968. Contains sixteen unrelated essays. Two, Joachim W. Storck's "Stifter und Rilke," and Richard Exner's "Hugo von Hofmannsthal zu Adalbert Stifter. Notizen und Entwürfe, vorläufige Chronik und Deutung," include hitherto unknown and unpublished material.

STRICH, FRITZ. "Adalbert Stifter und unsere Zeit." In *Der Dichter und die Zeit.* Berne: Francke, 1947, pp. 291–326.

WEIPPERT, GEORG. *Stifters Witiko: Vom Wesen des Politischen.* Posthumously published by Christian Thiel. Postscript by Theodor Pütz. Munich: R. Oldenbourg, 1967.

WIESE, BENNO VON. "Adalbert Stifter. Brigitta." In *Die deutsche Novelle von Goethe bis Kafka: Interpretationen.* Düsseldorf: Bagel, 1962, I, 196–212:347. (1st ed., 1956.)

———."Adalbert Stifter. Abdias." *Ibid.* II, 127–48: 349–50.

Index

(Includes investigators when the cited work does not appear in the Selected Bibliography.)

171